About this book

Dear Fifth Grader,

You have two topics you will study in Physical Science. They are Properties of Matter and Forces and Motion.

In Properties of Matter, you will make mixtures of punch to develop the "best" solution, separate the colors from a black marker, make and order solutions by their concentrations, determine the fastest way to dissolve a bouillon cube, along with many other things.

Some of the topics that are addressed in Properties of Matter are:
- matter is made up of particles too small to be seen
- matter has physical properties (volume, mass, movement)
- mixtures can be separated
- dissolving rates can be changed
- new substances are made when they are chemically combined

In Forces and Motion, you will explore the forces of magnetism, gravity, and friction. One of the experiences has you make an Air Glider that acts much like a hovercraft. You will move cars along a track to determine their position, direction, and speed. You will use helium balloons to explore balanced and unbalanced forces.

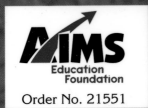

Education Foundation

Order No. 21551

The AIMS Education Foundation is a research and development organization dedicated to the improvement of the teaching and learning of mathematics and science through a meaningful integrated approach.

ISBN 978-1-932093-31-5

www.aimsedu.org • 888.733.2467

PHYSICAL SCIENCE
TABLE OF CONTENTS

HANDS-ON SAFE SCIENCE

Never work in a lab without a **responsible adult**.

If clothes catch fire, **stop, drop,** and **roll**.

Don't light matches around sulfur-sensitive people.

In a lab, **never** eat or drink anything.

PROTECT:
- your eyes- wear **goggles**
- your nose- **waft** to **whiff**
- your hands- wear **gloves**
- your feet- wear **closed shoes**
- your clothes- wear an **apron**
- your mouth- **don't taste**
- your hair- **tie it back** if it's long
- your face & skin- don't touch while handling materials

PREVENT:
- **fire**- never leave a heat source unattended
- **burns**- use mitts or tongs with hot materials
- **explosions**- never heat a closed container
- **confusion**- label all containers
- **cuts**- be careful with sharp instruments and always cut away from yourself and others
- **contamination**- use sealed containers for bacteria and mold and keep the lab **clean** and **neat**
- **damage**- only heat materials in **heat-resistant** containers
- **accidents**- never run, throw things, or play around in a lab
- **electrocution**- never submerge electrical appliances

DON'T TASTE

PREPARE:
- wash your hands
- know how a heat source works before using it
- know how to dispose of each type of waste properly
- follow all directions
- know what chemicals you are using & how to store them
- know the location of and how to use:
  - first aid kit
  - fire extinguishers
  - fire blankets

TOXIC

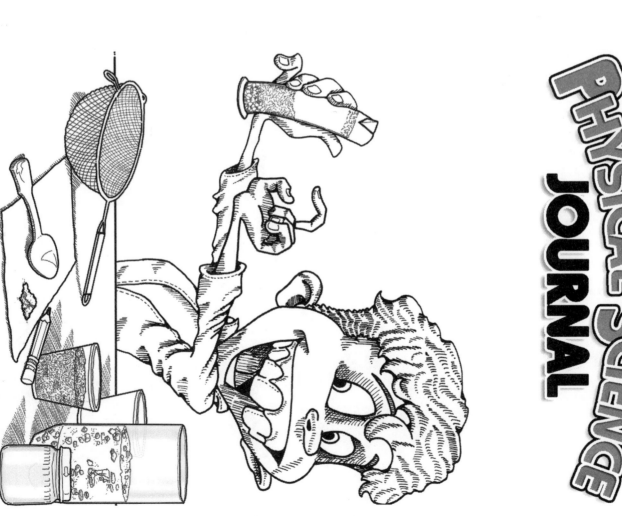

PHYSICAL SCIENCE JOURNAL

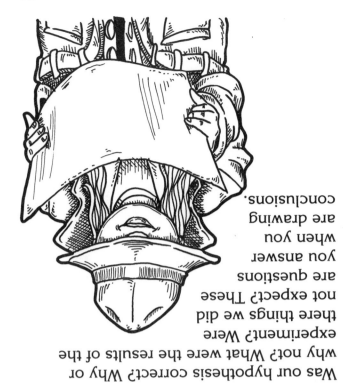

Drawing Conclusions: Generalizing the data.

Was our hypothesis correct? Why or why not? What were the results of the experiment? Were there things we did not expect? These are questions you answer when you are drawing conclusions.

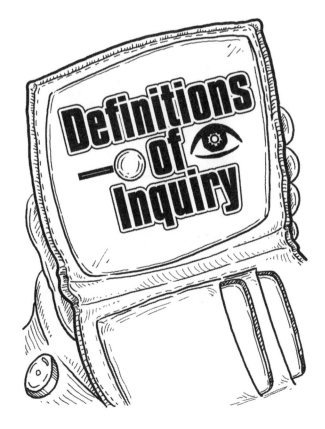

Observing: Using your five senses and other tools to explore properties of things.

What does it look like? How does it feel? What is its mass? How long is it? These are all questions you answer when you are making observations.

Communicating Results: Sharing the results of an experiment.

You can use words and/or writing to share your findings. You should tell what your hypothesis was, how you set up the experiment, and what you found.

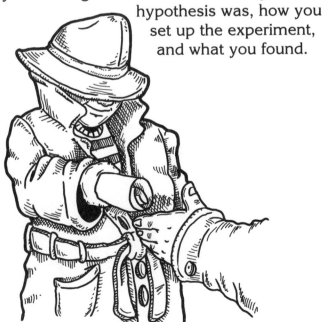

Definitions of Inquiry

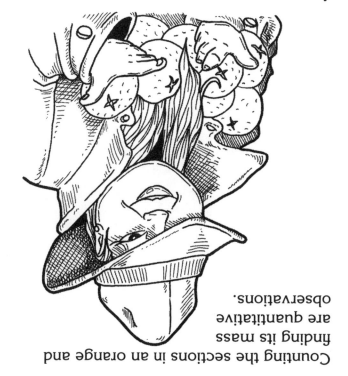

• *Quantitative* observations that look at the quantities of things. They use tools to make specific measurements.

Counting the sections in an orange and finding its mass are quantitative observations.

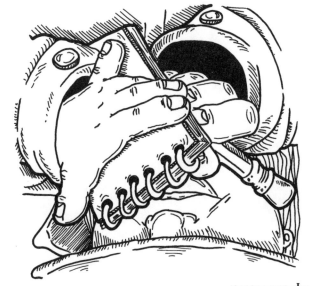

Recording: Writing the data you collect.

Line graphs, tables, and drawings are all ways to record data. Making models and recording descriptions in a science journal are other ways to record data. Good records are essential to a successful experiment.

Interpreting and Analyzing: Looking at the data to see what it tells you.

What does the line graph say about the data? How did the responding (dependent) variable change? What does the table tell us about our data? These are all questions you answer when you are analyzing.

• *Qualitative* observations that look at the qualities or characteristics of things. They use the senses—sight, taste, touch, hearing, and smell.

Observing the texture of an orange is a qualitative observation.

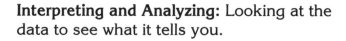

You might hypothesize that an increase in mass increases downhill speed based on your experiences riding bikes with friends. Hypotheses are often stated including both the manipulated and responding variables.

Hypothesis/Prediction: A statement about what you think the results of an experiment will be. This should be based on prior knowledge, not a wild guess.

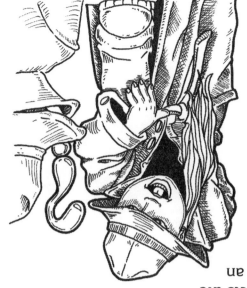

You could ask about how a change in mass affects the motion of an object.

Good questions are ones that you can find the answers to by designing experiments.

Questioning: Asking a question you can test and answer.

Identifying: Knowing the variables in the experiment.

- The *manipulated variable* is the thing you change to see what happens. This is also called the *independent variable*. It is graphed on the x-axis.
- The *responding variable* is the thing that might change because of what you did. This is also called the *dependent variable*. It is graphed on the y-axis.
- The *controlled variables* are the things that you need to keep the same.

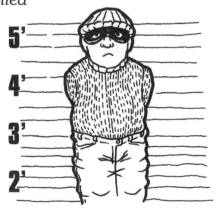

Measuring: Using tools like rulers, timers, and balances to find properties (length, mass, etc.) of things.

What is its mass? How long did it take? What is its capacity? These are all questions you answer when you are making measurements.

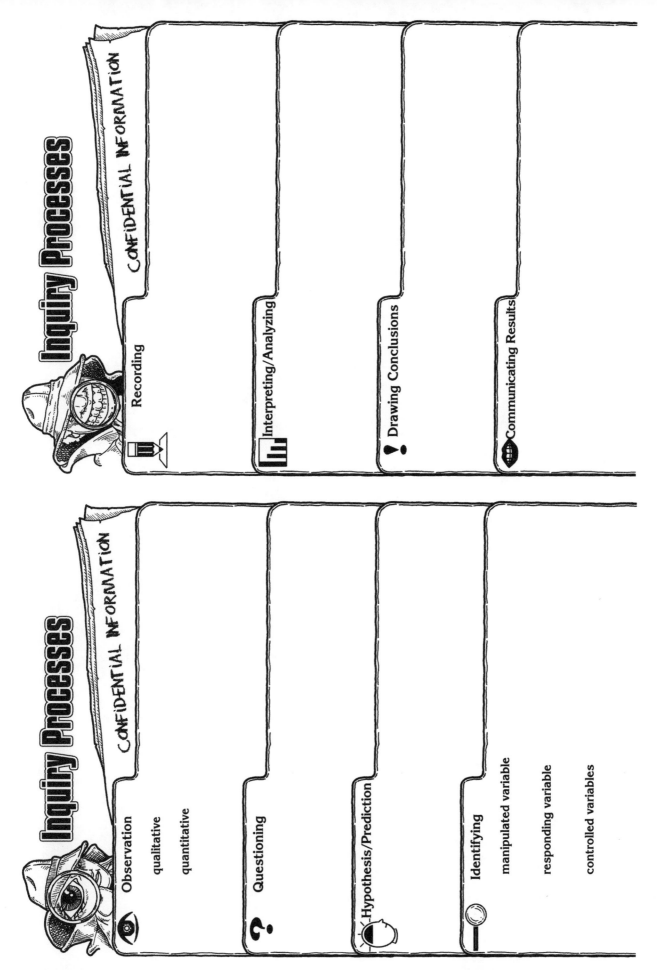

Inquiry Processes

CONFIDENTIAL INFORMATION

Recording

Interpreting/Analyzing

Drawing Conclusions

Communicating Results

Inquiry Processes

CONFIDENTIAL INFORMATION

Observation

qualitative

quantitative

Questioning

Hypothesis/Prediction

Identifying

manipulated variable

responding variable

controlled variables

The third grid represents a gas. Glue the last 16 circle punch-outs in this grid. The particles in a gas are well separated with no regular arrangement. The molecules vibrate and move freely at high speeds. Gases take the shape and volume of the container that they are in.

You will create models that show some of the characteristics of a solid, a liquid, and a gas. You will use circle punch-outs to represent the mass of each model.

Use what you learned in this book to record some of the characteristics and behaviors of each of the three states beside the models you just created.

A Matter of States

The three most common states of matter are solids, liquids, and gases. All matter is made up of molecules. All molecules vibrate or move and have space between them. The type of movement and space determine the state of the matter.

This model shows that the molecules in solids are tightly packed together and are usually in a regular pattern with little free space between them. The molecules in a solid vibrate but generally do not move from place to place. Solids keep a set volume and shape.

Look at the three area grids on the *A Matter of States* page. Label the grid with the smallest area a solid. You will need to glue a circle punch-out in each section of the grid.

Select the grid with the next largest area, and label it a liquid. Glue 16 circle punch-outs in the grid, but do not put them into any pattern. The molecules in a liquid are fairly close together, but have no special arrangement. The molecules in a liquid vibrate and slide past each other. Liquids take the shape of the container that they are in.

The first thing you will need to do is to make sure you have 48 circle punch-outs. You will use 16 circle punch-outs for each model.

A Matter of States

(State) _____

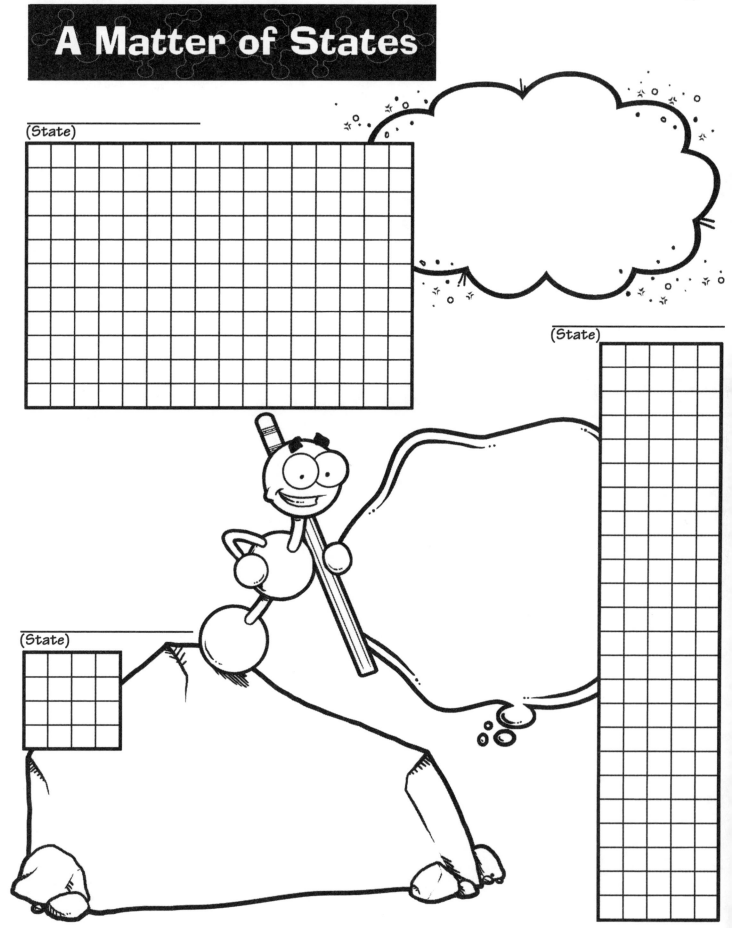

(State)

(State)

22

Make **Room** for ME!
Part 1

1. Pour 50 mL of water into a graduated container.

2. Pour 50 mL of water into a second graduated container.

3. Predict the volume of the combined liquids. _____ mL

4. Combine the two liquids. Record the volume of the combined liquids. _____ mL

5. Shade the graduated container in the diagram.

6. Empty the graduated container.

7. Repeat the above procedure using isopropyl alcohol. Record the volume of the combined liquids. _____ mL

8. Follow the same procedure using 50 mL of water and 50 mL of isopropyl alcohol. Record the volume of the combined liquids. _____mL

Explain this result.

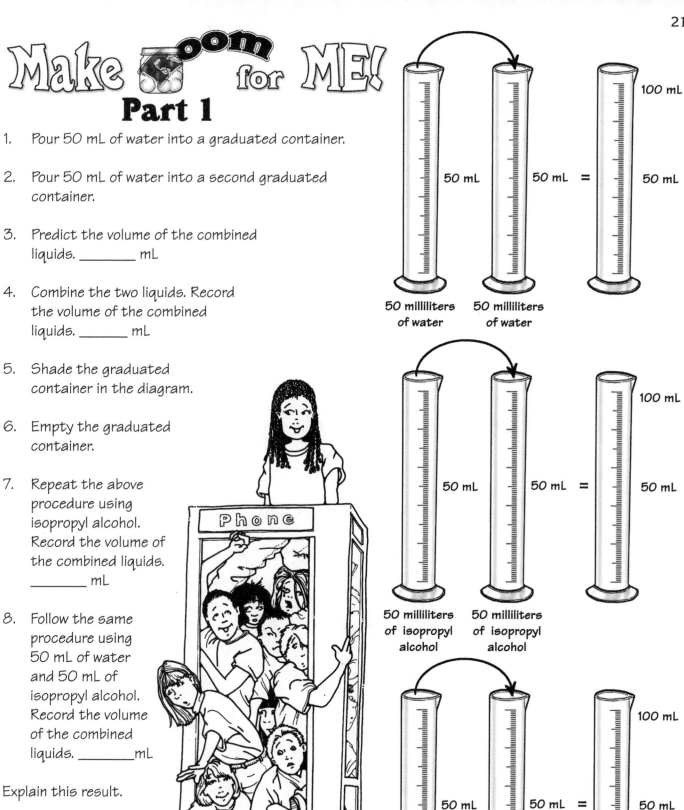

50 mL   50 mL   =   100 mL
                        50 mL

50 milliliters   50 milliliters
of water   of water

50 mL   50 mL   =   100 mL
                        50 mL

50 milliliters   50 milliliters
of isopropyl   of isopropyl
alcohol   alcohol

50 mL   50 mL   =   100 mL
                        50 mL

50 milliliters   50 milliliters
of water   of alcohol

Make Zoom for ME! Part 2

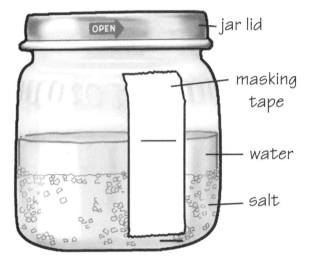

baby food jar

1. Fill a graduated container 1/3 full of rock salt.

2. Add water to a level 2-3 cm above the level of the rock salt. Mark the level of water and salt mixture on the masking tape.

3. Predict the level after shaking.
   _____ above the line
   _____ on the line
   _____ below the line

4. Cover the container with the jar lid. Shake the container for at least one minute.

5. Record the results.
   _____ above the line
   _____ on the line
   _____ below the line

How do you explain the results?

Make  oom for ME! Part 3

1. Using the jar lid as a "scoop," predict how many scoops it will take to fill a baby food jar with marbles.

Prediction

_____ Scoops

   Fill the container with marbles. Record the number of scoops. Leave the marbles in the jar.

Measurement

_____ Scoops

2. Predict how many scoops it will take to fill the container with popcorn.

Prediction

_____ Scoops

   Add the popcorn to the container. Record the number of scoops. Leave the popcorn in the container.

Measurement

_____ Scoops

3. Predict how many scoops it will take to fill the container with sand.

Prediction

_____ Scoops

   Add the sand to the container. Record the number of scoops.

Measurement

_____ Scoops

4. Make a drawing of your container and its contents.

5. Graph the actual measurements for each item added to the container.

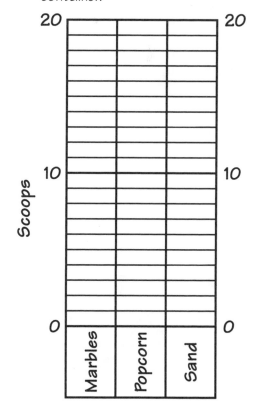

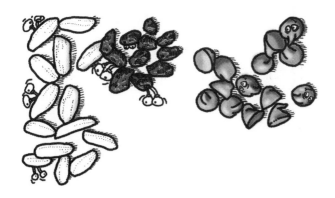

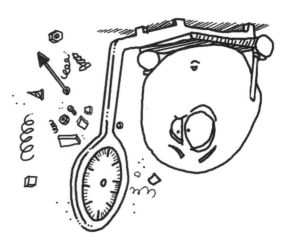

Mixtures can be separated. You can separate the trail mix into piles of peanuts, raisins, and chocolate chips. You could separate the sugar from the water by letting the water evaporate. The sugar would be left in the glass. Not all mixtures are so easy to separate. Sometimes complicated procedures must be used.

Matter refers to all the materials found in nature. Matter is made up of atoms. It takes up space and has weight. Matter can be classified into three groups: elements, compounds, and mixtures.

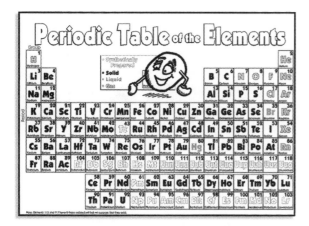

All matter is made up of these 100 plus elements and their combinations. (Living things and most materials are made up of just a few elements.) Chemistry is the study of these elements and their combinations.

IN THE

OF THINGS

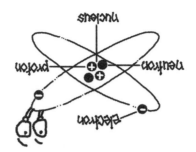

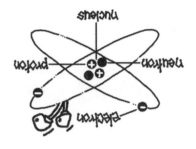

You make mixtures when you cook. If you and a friend were to each make a trail mix, you might like more peanuts than raisins. Your friend might like more chocolate chips than peanuts. You are making a mixture.

Elements are pure substances. This means that every sample of an element is just like every other sample of it. Elements cannot easily be broken down into simpler substances.

When you drink iced tea, you are drinking a mixture. When you eat a bowl of breakfast cereal with milk, you are eating a mixture. When you dig up a handful of soil, you are holding a mixture.

Elements are those things like carbon, oxygen, gold, silver, and iron. There are over 100 known elements. These elements are arranged in a chart called the Periodic Table of Elements.

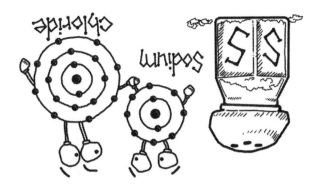

Regular table salt is a compound made up of two elements: one part sodium (Na) and one part chloride (Cl). The properties of a compound are different than the properties of the elements that make them up. For example, the sodium and chloride that make up salt are poisonous elements. When they are chemically combined, they produce salt, something we all eat.

Water is a compound. It is made up of two parts hydrogen (H) and one part oxygen (O). Every sample of pure water will be just the same as every other sample of pure water. Some other common compounds are salt and sugar.

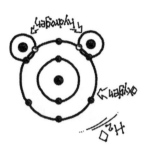

Mixtures are combinations of elements or compounds in any proportion. Think about mixing sugar and water. You can have a mixture that has a lot of sugar or a little bit of sugar in the water.

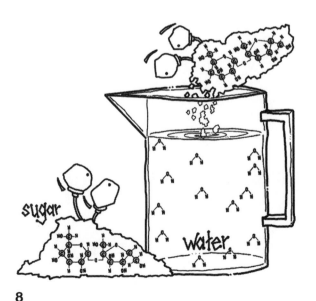

Compounds are also pure substances. They are made up of two or more elements. When elements are combined chemically in a fixed ratio, they produce new substances.

39

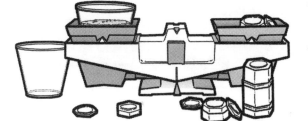

Messing with Mixtures

Find the mass of: mixture and cup _____

－   empty cup _____

_____

                              mixture _____

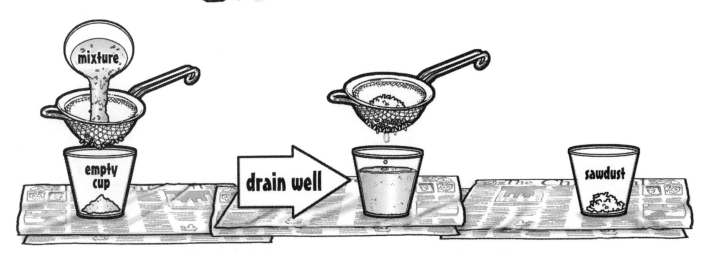

drain well

Find the mass of: sawdust and cup _____

－   empty cup _____

_____

                              sawdust _____

Describe ideas about how to separate the remaining ingredients.

Messing with Mixtures

Day 2

Find the mass of:

plaster of Paris and cup _____

empty cup _____

_____

plaster of Paris _____

Describe ideas about how to separate the remaining ingredients.

How long do you think it is going to take for the water to evaporate?

What do you think is going to be left in the cup after the water is gone?

Find the mass of:

sugar and cup _____

empty cup _____

_____

sugar _____

plaster of Paris _____

sawdust _____

water _____

+ sugar _____

_____

total _____

Does the total mass of the component mixtures equal the mass you had at the beginning of the activity? Explain.

Chromatographic Circles

What did you observe?

Record the order of the colors you see from first to last.

Color in your
final design.

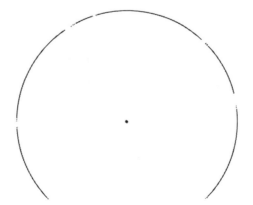

Different companies
use different pigments
to make the black ink
we see in markers.

The name comes from the Greek
words chroma which means color,
and graph which means to write.

Water-soluble pigments are different
from permanent ink pigments.

Chromatography is one method
used to separate the components
of a mixture.

12

1

The different pigments in the ink have different solubility in water. That means they have different levels of attraction for the moving water and attraction to the filter paper.

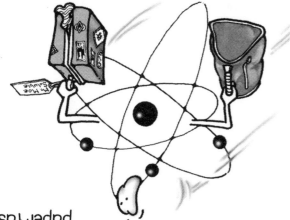

The pigments that have a greater attraction for the water are more soluble and spend more time in the water. These are the colors that travel up the paper faster.

The spot of ink is not in the water; it is just above the water. The water moves up the strip by the process of capillary action (like a wick) and is able to dissolve the components in the ink spot.

The pigments, which have less attraction for water, are less soluble, and travel up the filter paper more slowly.

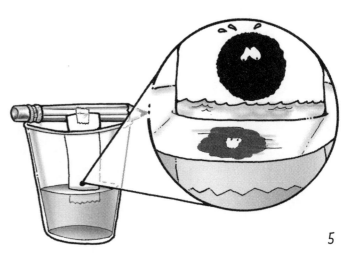

8

5

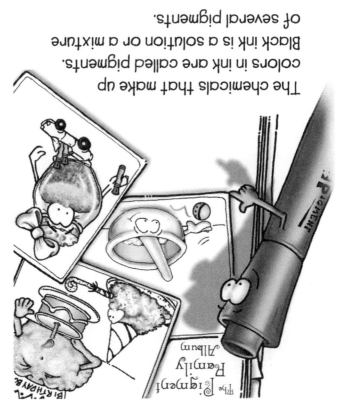

The chemicals that make up colors in ink are called pigments. Black ink is a solution or a mixture of several pigments.

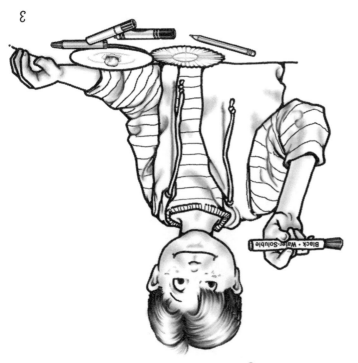

We used paper chromatography to separate the black inks in our investigation.

Paper chromatography uses strips of filter paper. The coffee filter paper you used is similar to the type of filter paper used in traditional paper chromatography. A spot of ink is placed on the strip. The strips are then suspended so that just the tip of the paper is in the water.

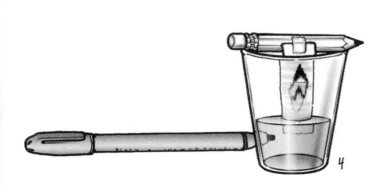

4

If you have enough time and there are differences in the solubility of the pigments, the pigments can be completely separated.

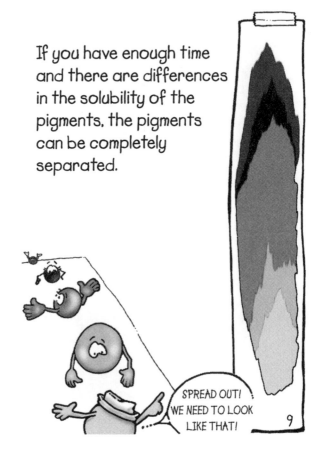

SPREAD OUT! WE NEED TO LOOK LIKE THAT!

9

Metal Detector

Wrap the magnet in plastic wrap.

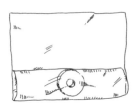

Tie the ends of the plastic wrap around the end of your pencil.

List the objects hidden in your "beach bag."

Check (✓) the ones you predict will be attracted by the magnet.

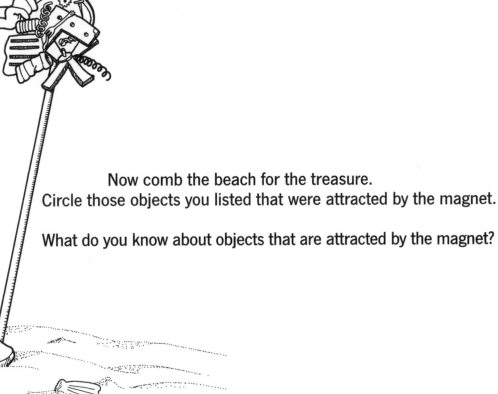

Now comb the beach for the treasure.
Circle those objects you listed that were attracted by the magnet.

What do you know about objects that are attracted by the magnet?

Involving Dissolving

1. **Use your own words to define a solution, a solvent, and solute.**

	water	rubbing alcohol
kosher salt	$\frac{1}{2}$ tsp	$\frac{1}{2}$ tsp
alum	$\frac{1}{2}$ tsp	$\frac{1}{2}$ tsp
Epsom salt	$\frac{1}{2}$ tsp	$\frac{1}{2}$ tsp

2. **Describe how salt is a solute in this investigation.**

3. **Which solvent seemed to be able to hold the most solute?**

4. **Water is called the universal solvent. From what you learned in this investigation, explain why this is true.**

SEA SALT

Staple bag here

Record your data:

Total number of dots = _____

Number of red dots = _____

Number of blue dots = _____

Use the count of your red dots to record your data in parts per thousand (ppt).

SEA SALT

There are 1000 squares in this grid. Use two colors to show the average amount of salt in ocean water.

The average salinity of ocean water is 35 ppt.

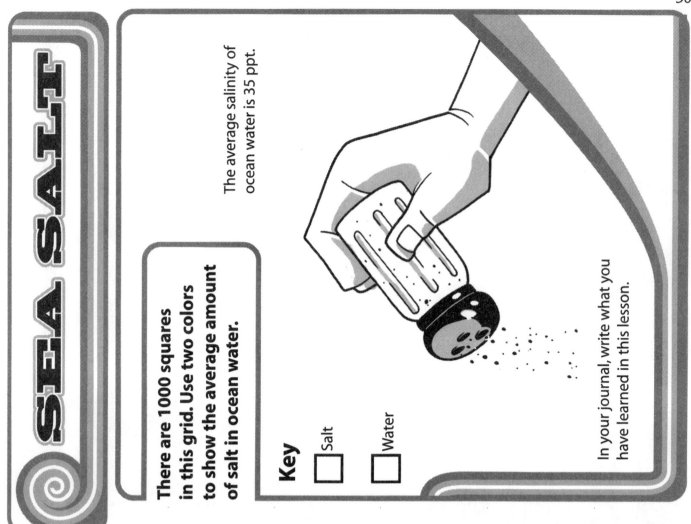

Key

☐ Salt

☐ Water

In your journal, write what you have learned in this lesson.

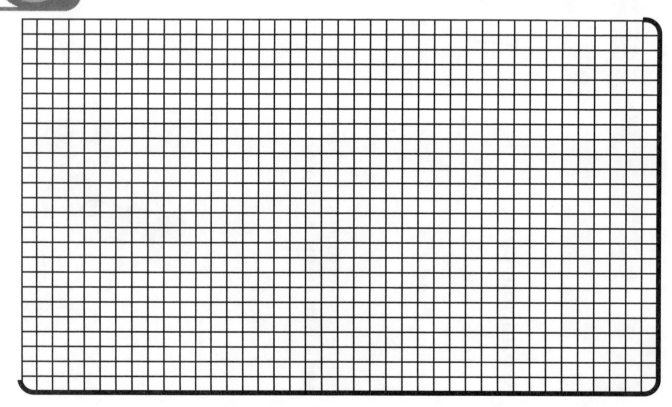

SEA SALT

Use one color to shade in arid areas. Use another color to shade in tropical areas. Which areas of ocean water do you think have the higher salinity rates? Why?

7

In science a *solution* has a specific meaning. For something to be a solution, the following things must be true:

- two or more materials are mixed together
- the materials are evenly distributed
- the materials stay mixed

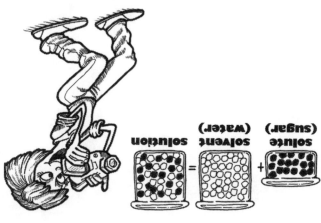

Pressure can change the solvent. When you increase the pressure, you can usually dissolve more gas in a liquid. Think about a soda can. The soda stays fizzy because the contents of the can are under pressure. If you leave a soda open for too long, it goes flat.

The structure of the substance can affect how soluble it is. Some substances dissolve easier in one kind of substance than another. Sugar dissolves easily in water. Oil does not dissolve easily in water. Water has a low solubility when it comes to oil.

SOLVING SOLUTIONS

8

1

The *solubility* of solutions can be changed by different things. *Solubility* is the ability of the solvent (water) to dissolve the solute (sugar).

A simple solution has two parts. One of them is called the *solute*. The solute is the substance to be dissolved (e.g., sugar). The other is the *solvent*. The solvent is the one doing the dissolving (e.g., water). There is usually more solvent than solute in a solution.

Temperature can increase the ability of the solvent to hold more solute. You can dissolve more sugar in hot water than in cold water.

Almost anything can be a solution. Solutions can be solids dissolved in liquids. Salt water is this kind of solution. They can also be gases dissolved in liquids. Soda is this kind of solution. They can be gases in other gases and liquids in liquids. Solids mixed with other solids are usually called mixtures, not solutions.

84

Souper SOLUBILITY
STIRRING THINGS UP

Introduction

This investigation will explore how the rate of stirring affects how quickly a bouillon cube dissolves. Stirring is the manipulated (independent) variable in this investigation.

These are some of the variables you will need to control

Size of the cups
Amount of water
Temperature of the water

Number of bouillon cubes
What you stir with

The time it takes to dissolve will be the responding (dependent) variable.

Materials

3 clear graduated cups, 9 oz
3 bouillon cubes
1 craft stick
1 thermometer

Design of the Investigation

1. Add 250 mL of water to each of the cups.
2. Find the temperature of the water in each cup using the thermometer.
3. Add a bouillon cube to cup one and record the time it was added. Record the time it appears to be completely dissolved. Record all data in the table.
4. Add a bouillon cube to cup two and record the time it was added. Use the craft stick to slowly stir the contents of the cup. Use a circular motion. Record the time it appears to be completely dissolved. Record all data in the table.
5. Add a bouillon cube to cup three and record the time it was added. Use the craft stick to quickly stir the contents of the cup. Use a circular motion. Record the time it appears to be completely dissolved. Record all data in the table.

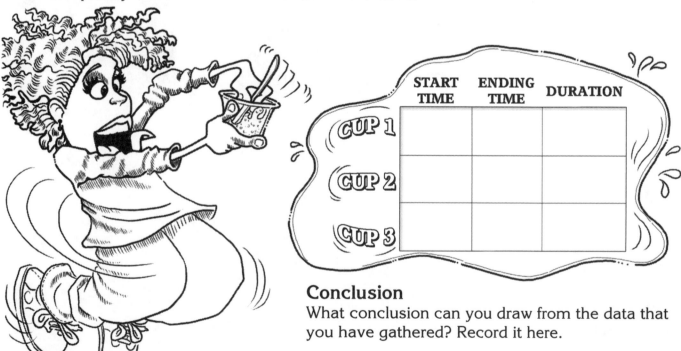

	START TIME	ENDING TIME	DURATION
CUP 1			
CUP 2			
CUP 3			

Conclusion

What conclusion can you draw from the data that you have gathered? Record it here.

Souper SOLUBILITY
THE HEAT IS ON!

Introduction to the Investigation
This investigation will explore how temperature affects how quickly a bouillon cube dissolves. What is the manipulated (independent) variable in this investigation?

These are some of the variables you will need to control:

Size of the cups   Number of bouillon cubes
Amount of water   What you stir with
The rate at which you stir

What is the responding (dependent) variable in this investigation?

Materials

3 clear graduated cups, 9 oz
3 bouillon cubes
1 craft stick
thermometer
source for hot water

Design of the Investigation
1. You will be adding 250 mL of water to each of the cups. In the first cup, the beginning temperature needs to be approximately 15° Celsius. Add the bouillon and use the craft stick to stir in a constant motion. Record the time you added the bouillon cube and the time it appears to be completely dissolved.
2. Repeat the procedure using water at approximately 30°C for cup two.
3. Repeat the procedure using water at approximately 45°C for cup three.

	START TIME	ENDING TIME	DURATION
CUP 1			
CUP 2			
CUP 3			

Conclusion
What conclusion can you draw from the data that you have gathered? Record it here.

Souper SOLUBILITY

Question to be the investigated

What is the manipulated (independent) variable?

What are the variables you will need to control?

What is the responding (dependent) variable in this investigation?

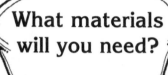

What materials will you need?

What will the design of you investigation look like?

Conclusion

What conclusion can you draw from the data that you have gathered? Record it here.

Product Testing

Mix each formula with 40 mL of borax solution.

FORMULA A
20 mL glue
_____ %
20 mL water
_____ %

FORMULA B
30 mL glue
_____ %
10 mL water
_____ %

FORMULA C
40 mL glue
_____ %
0 mL water
_____ %

Observation of
glue solutions

A.

B.

C.

Observation of
borax solutions

A.

B.

C.

Observation of
the Glubber

A.

B.

C.

1. How are the solutions the same?

2. How are the solutions different?

3. What happened when you mixed the two solutions?

Product Testing

Record your data from each test.

	Formula A	Formula B	Formula C
Bounce Test			
Shape Retention Test			
Imprint Test			
Stretch Test			
Print Transfer Test			

Product Testing

Give a written summary on which formula you recommend based on the results of the experiments.

Product Testing
Recommendation

Formula ____

Design an ad to sell your product. Use the properties of the Glubber as selling features.

Well Recording Sheet

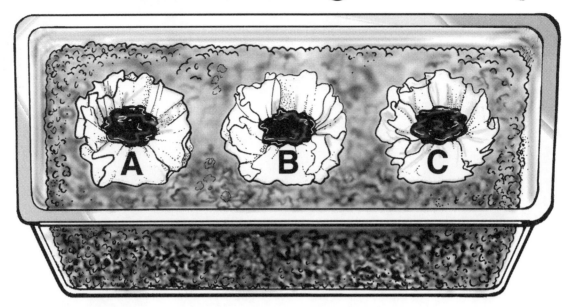

Beginning water samples. (Tape or glue your litmus paper strips to each well below.)

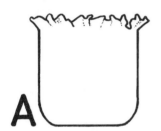 A

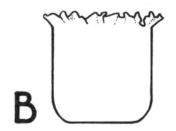 B

 C

Water samples after an acid rain. (Vinegar)

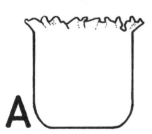 A

 B

 C

Water samples after a fertilizer spill. (Window cleaner or diluted ammonia)

 A

 B

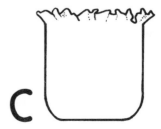 C

Explain your results in your Science Journal.

2

Make observations

Perform the experiment (you might need to do this several times)

Record your observations

Interpret your results

Draw conclusions

Toddlers learn by answering their own questions. They may not be able to speak, but they still have questions. They see an event that excites their curiosity. They make up experiments to learn how it works.

When you are doing experiments, pay attention to each of these steps. They can help you find the answers to your questions.

Scientific Inquiry: INQUIRING MINDS

Toddlers are doing their own type of scientific inquiry. It begins with asking a question. Scientists do the same thing as toddlers. They ask good questions, and they work to find the answers.

What questions could the toddlers be exploring? Does the cup always hit the floor? Does it always make that noise? Does the cup always fall down?

The scientific method is one way to ask and answer questions.

You have probably seen one-year-olds knock cups off tables. Someone picks them up. What do the toddlers do? They knock them off again and again. Usually they will keep this up longer than the other persons want to pick them up.

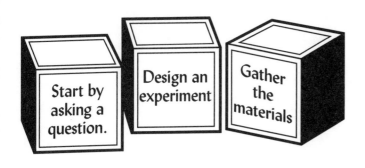

Start by asking a question.

Design an experiment

Gather the materials

3

Asking questions and searching for answers!

What is at the heart of scientific inquiry?

WHAT WOULD HAPPEN IF ...?

Where do these questions come from? They usually come from things that you do or see. Sometimes after you have done an experiment in class, you might say, "What would happen if ...?"

Think about whether your question is one that you can test. If it is, you are ready to begin designing your experiment.

Scientific Inquiry:
ASKING QUESTIONS

© 2006 AIMS Education Foundation

You will have several controlled variables.

- All tomato plants should be the same kind.
- They should all get the same amount of light.
- They should all get the same amount of water.
- They should all be planted in the same kind of dirt.
- They should all be planted in the same type of pot.

There are three types of variables: manipulated, responding, and controlled.

Manipulated: this is the thing YOU change to see what happens

Responding: this is the thing that might change because of what you did

Controlled: these are the things that you need to keep the same in the experiment.

See, designing an experiment is hard work, but it is fun! And you find out the answers to your questions.

Scientific Inquiry:
IDENTIFYING THE VARIABLES

Designing an experiment may not be as easy as it sounds. You need to think about variables. Variables are things that will affect your experiment.

118

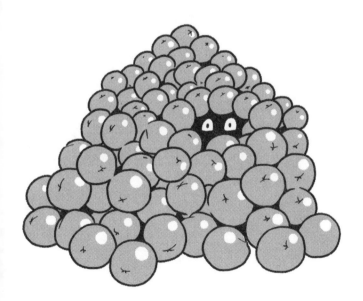

Your manipulated variable is the amount of fertilizer you will test. You will want to come up with different amounts. (0 mL, 2 mL, 4 mL, and so on)

How much fertilizer is best for your tomatoes?

Let's say you came up with this question to test.

Your responding variable will be how many tomatoes your plants produce.

The rule is: You only have one manipulated variable in an experiment. If you use more than one, you may not know which one is causing a change.

6

3

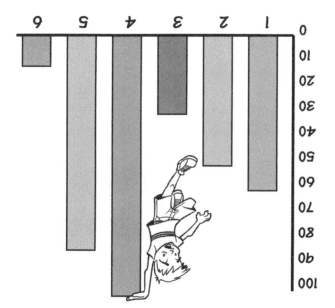

When the data include numbers and measurements, they can be organized and displayed in tables and graphs. You will often see patterns in the tables and graphs that you might have missed if you hadn't used them.

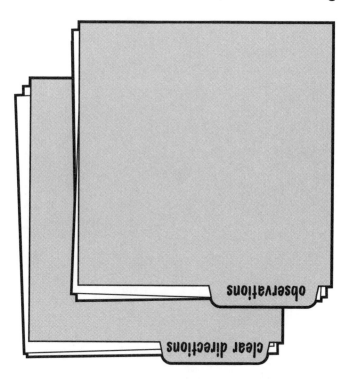

It is important that you keep good records of your experiment. These records include:

clear directions

observations

When good records are kept, they are easier to analyze. You are then ready to interpret the results and draw conclusions.

Scientific Inquiry: KEEPING GOOD RECORDS

8

1

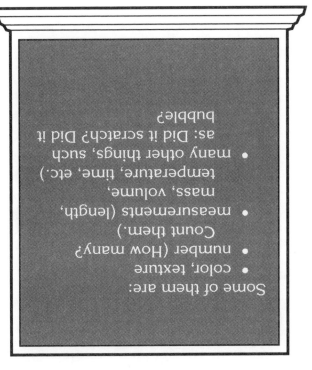

Some of them are:
- color, texture
- number (How many? Count them.)
- measurements (length, mass, volume, temperature, time, etc.)
- many other things, such as: Did it scratch? Did it bubble?

Your records need to include your observations. What observations should you include? There are many things that you could observe.

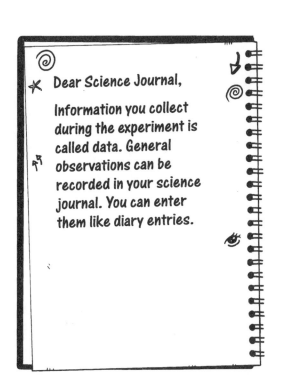

Dear Science Journal,

Information you collect during the experiment is called data. General observations can be recorded in your science journal. You can enter them like diary entries.

You need clear directions so that others can do your experiment. If they follow your directions, they should get similar results. If they don't get similar results, you need to find out why.

Scientific Inquiry: DEALING WITH RESULTS

You might think that once you have gathered the data and made a graph that the experiment is over.

IT'S NOT?

If that were true, you might not know the answer to the question you asked.

Now you can share your results with others. They may have questions for you. They may want to see if they get the same results as you did. Since you kept good records, they should be able to do the experiment just like you did.

You now need to interpret the results. What do your data tell you? You can use the results to draw conclusions. You might even want to form a hypothesis and do further testing.

HOW DOES IT LOOK?

HMM... I NEED TO DO SOME MORE TESTS.

What is the cause?
The length of the pendulum

What is the effect?
The number
of swings in a
minute

Here's a hypothesis: If I lengthen a pendulum, it will swing fewer times in a minute.

WILD GUESSES
WITH
THE AMAZING
LARRY

Sometimes in science, you are asked to predict or hypothesize about some event and you do not have a clue. In these cases, you are making a wild guess. So, what are the differences in wild guesses, predictions, and hypothesis making?

The cause is the manipulated variable or independent variable. The effect is the responding variable or dependent variable. Notice that the hypothesis includes both of them. Hypotheses are always made after you have had some experience investigating the situation.

My Hypothesis

by
The Amazing
LARRY

Scientific Inquiry:
HYPOTHESIZING

In science, you may observe that a weak magnet attracts three paper clips. You predict that a stronger magnet will pick up more. You are applying what you know to another situation.

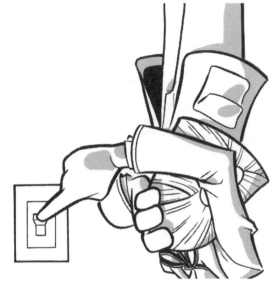

A prediction is more than a guess. You apply something you know to the situation. You predict all the time without thinking much about it. You predict that the light will turn on when you flip a switch.

A hypothesis is even more sophisticated. A hypothesis is a prediction about how variables are related. Hypotheses are always testable. They test cause and effect relationships.

CAUSE AND EFFECT: A RELATIONSHIP

A wild guess is just that—a guess. You don't have any information on which to base your answer. If you were asked how many razzmalites would fit in a jar, you would just have to guess. You wouldn't know what a razzmalite is. You wouldn't know how big it is. Nor would you know how big the jar is.

2

The amount of friction depends on the kinds of surfaces and how hard they are pressing against each other. Think about two rough surfaces pressed hard together—sandpaper and a rough block of wood. To move one across the other will be much harder than two smooth surfaces like a mirror and an ice cube.

DOWN

UP

Gravity is a force you know well. If you stumble, what happens? You fall. Which way do you fall? You don't fall up, you fall down! Gravity is the attraction between two objects. It is considered to be a non-contact force because the objects do not have to be touching each other.

If you want something to stay in place and not move about easily, friction can be your friend.

WHEW !!

Brake

But sometimes friction can be aggravating. There is no surface that can be completely free of friction. Even the smoothest surfaces have slight imperfections.

FORMIDABLE

FORCES

What kinds of forces are there? You may be surprised to find that you are familiar with several of them. Think about how each of these forces affects motion.

Magnetism is like gravity in that its strength is determined by distance. The closer the magnetic objects are, the greater the force. The further they are from each other, the weaker it is. Magnetism is a non-contact force. The magnets don't have to touch in order to affect each other.

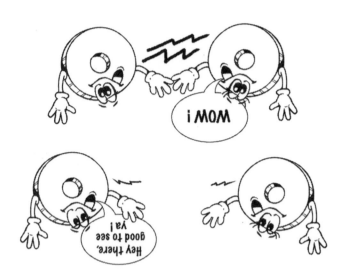

Magnetism is another force. It belongs in a category called electromagnetic forces. This is a force of attraction and repulsion. Think of two magnets. If you put like poles together, they repel each other. When unlike poles are put together, they are attracted to each other. A magnetic force can also exist between a magnet and an object that contains iron.

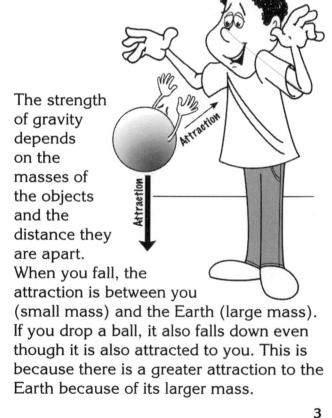

I find you truly repelling!

It's my magnetic personality!

If you would just turn and look at me, I know you'd be attracted.

Another force is **friction.** Friction is a contact force. Friction is a resistance to movement. Even though there are many types of friction, sliding friction is an easy example to help us understand it. Whenever two surfaces rub against each other, there is sliding friction. When you slide a book across a desk or move a chair across the floor, friction is at work. The friction between the two surfaces makes it harder to move the object.

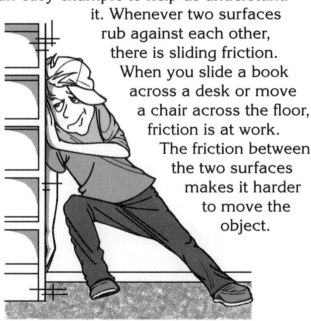

The strength of gravity depends on the masses of the objects and the distance they are apart. When you fall, the attraction is between you (small mass) and the Earth (large mass). If you drop a ball, it also falls down even though it is also attracted to you. This is because there is a greater attraction to the Earth because of its larger mass.

There is good news and bad news about friction. The good news is that friction is sometimes helpful. Think about the brakes on your bicycle or on your roller blades. You want those surfaces to press together enough to stop you. That's when friction is good.

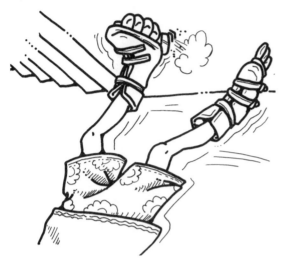

Have you ever taken your shoes off and slid in your socks on a smooth floor? It's fun to see how far you can slide. What would happen if you tried to slide on a floor covered with carpet? Why can't you slide?

It's bad news when you are trying to drag something that is very heavy across a rough surface. The friction will make your job much harder.

Friction

There is a powerful force at work that keeps you from going the direction you want to go. This force is called friction. It is a force that happens when two surfaces come in contact with each other—like your socks on the floor.

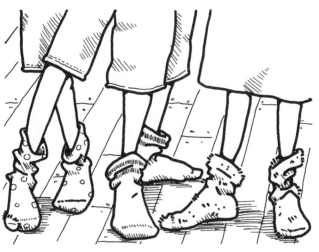

When two surfaces are touching, there might be a lot of friction or there might be just a little friction. It depends on two things.

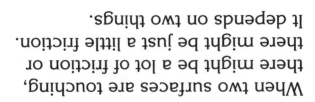

1. It depends on what the surfaces are made of. Think about ice sliding on a sheet of glass. Both of these surfaces are very smooth so they do not have much friction. But sandpaper sliding on a piece of carpet has a lot of friction because of their rough surfaces.

2. The other thing that affects friction is how hard the two surfaces are pressing together. Try this: Press the palms of your hands together and gently rub them back and forth. Now press your hands together harder and rub them back and forth. Which way produced more friction? The hard rub, right? So the harder things are pressed together, the greater the friction will be.

Forceful Friction

Friction is a force that is present when an object moves across a surface. This force acts in the opposite direction of the motion. The harder an object is to move, the greater the friction present.

METHOD 1
Place a ring magnet at the start of the path and another ring magnet directly below the first, underneath the path so that the two magnets attract each other. With two helpers holding the path above your desk, move the top magnet along the path using the bottom magnet.

METHOD 2
Next, put the path in a plastic sheet protector and repeat this process.

METHOD 3
Finally, place the path on top of a thin book and repeat the above process.

Forceful Friction

Which of the methods had the most friction?

Which had the least amount of friction?

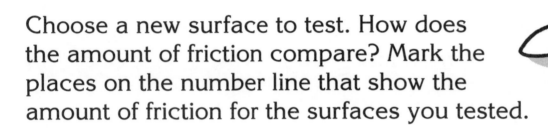

How could you tell?

Choose a new surface to test. How does the amount of friction compare? Mark the places on the number line that show the amount of friction for the surfaces you tested.

A. path paper

B. sheet protector

C. book

D. _____
    YOUR CHOICE

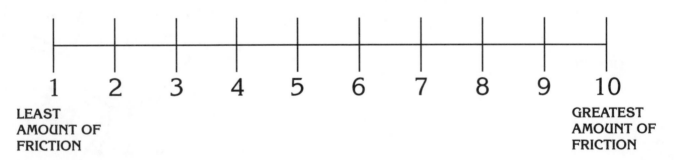

1   2   3   4   5   6   7   8   9   10

LEAST AMOUNT OF FRICTION

GREATEST AMOUNT OF FRICTION

A-maze-ing Magnets

Exploration:

1. Place your two magnets flat on your desk. Move one magnet slowly toward the other. Describe what happens.

2. Turn one of the magnets over and repeat the process. Describe what happens.

3. Place one magnet on your desk and hold the other one directly above it. Slowly move the magnet in your hand toward the one on the table. Describe what happens.

4. Turn one of the magnets over and repeat the above process. Describe what happens.

5. Continue to play with your magnets and try different things. Can you cause one of the magnets to go in a circle without touching it? Can you make one of the magnets flip? How about partially suspending one of the magnets? Describe your additional discoveries below.

A-maze-ing Magnets

Questions:

1. What did you learn about magnetic attraction from your explorations?

2. What did you learn about magnetic repulsion from your explorations?

3. Based on the things you did, which part of a ring magnet has the strongest magnetic field? Explain why you think this.

4. List several things that you discovered about magnets that you did not know until today.

5. What do all of these discoveries tell you about magnets and their properties?

Now that you have experimented with your magnets, you have a challenge. Using your two magnets, direct one of them through the maze on the next page without touching this magnet. Try to stay between the lines as much as possible.

Brick Slide

How easily can a brick be pulled across different surfaces?

Use words, rubbings, and/or pictures to describe the surface. Record the length of stretch on the sign.

It's 2600 BC and you are building a pyramid in Egypt. You need to pull huge blocks of rock from the quarry to the building site. You are going to use a brick to test the job ahead of you with a brick.

Length of Stretch

Surface:

Length of Stretch

Surface:

Surface:

Length of Stretch

Surface:

Length of Stretch

Order the surfaces from easiest (least stretch) to most difficult (most stretch).

_____

_____

_____

_____

_____

Across which surface would you prefer to pull your brick? Why?

Length of Stretch

Surface:

© 2006 AIMS Education Foundation

Slip, Sliding Away

How can we reduce friction?

Lubricant	Slide Times									Average Times*

*Color the high and low times for each lubricant. Write the remaining number, the median average, in the last column.

Inclined Plane

Surface:

Length:

Height:

Sliding Object

Kind:

Mass:

Slip, Sliding Away

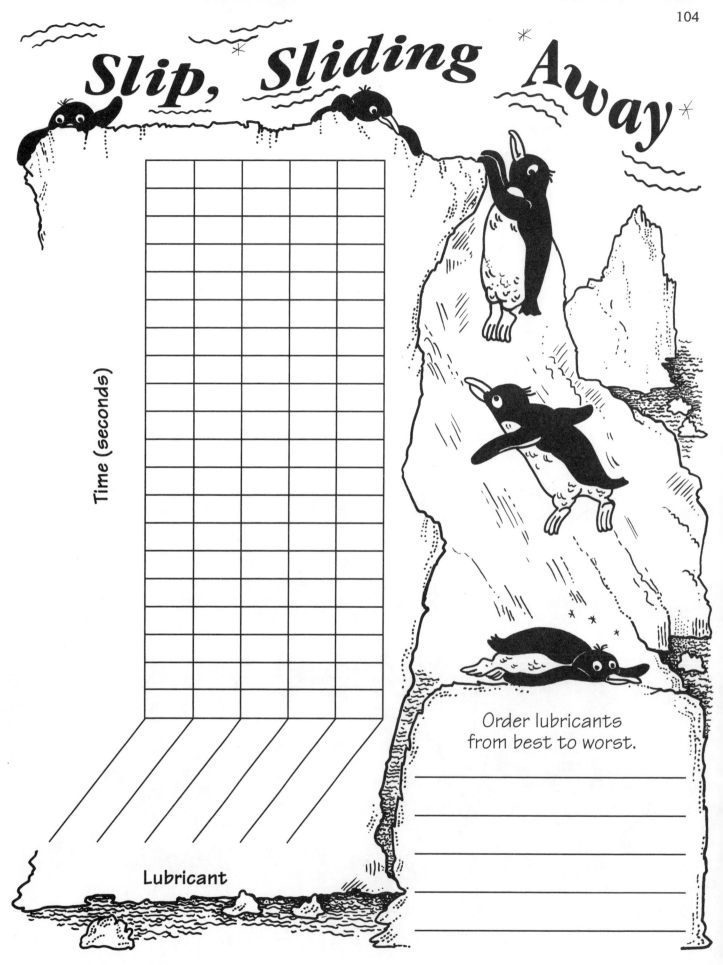

Time (seconds)

Lubricant

Order lubricants from best to worst.

_____

_____

_____

_____

_____

1. Hold your elbow tight to your side and use your fingertip to push the CD across a tabletop as far as possible.

2. Record the straight line distance traveled by the CD. Do three trials and average the results.

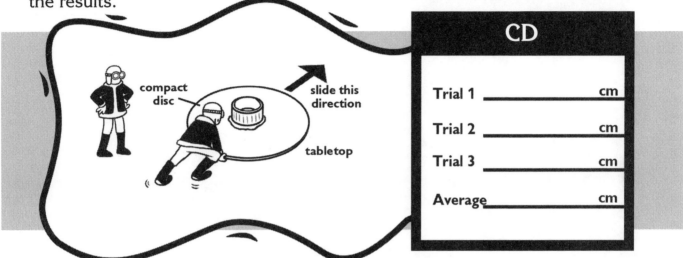

compact disc

slide this direction

tabletop

CD

Trial 1		cm
Trial 2		cm
Trial 3		cm
Average		cm

3. Repeat the procedure with the Air Glider.

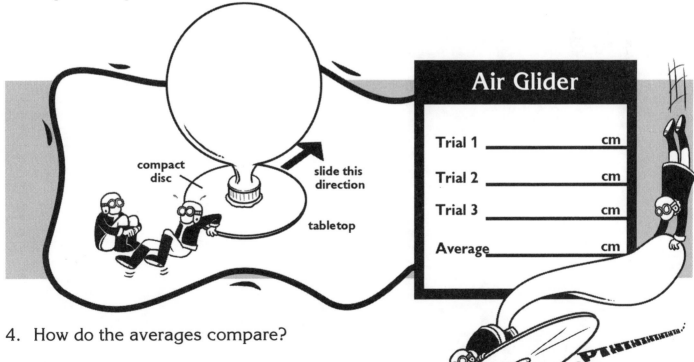

compact disc

slide this direction

tabletop

Air Glider

Trial 1		cm
Trial 2		cm
Trial 3		cm
Average		cm

4. How do the averages compare?

5. In your Science Journal, explain how the Air Glider works.

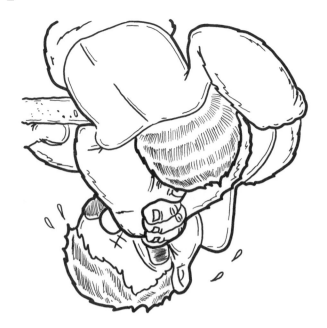

Ug beat Squirl, but it took some effort. Ug and Squirl had a balanced force for part of the match. At the point Ug was able to pin Squirl, he exerted an unbalance force.

A force can be thought of as a push or pull. A force transfers energy to an object. If the force is great enough, it can cause an object to start moving, stop moving, or change its motion. Hoam, the mother in the prehistoric Lea family, understood how to apply forces to move things. Her husband Ug and son Squirl were not quite as knowledgeable in this area. We will use them to learn about balanced and unbalanced forces.

Did Hoam and Ug have a balanced or unbalanced force in their match? Study the following diagrams on the next page. Decide which set of arrows represent the forces for each diagram. A small arrow and a large arrow indicate an unbalanced force. The arrows point in the direction the force is being applied. Circle the pair of arrows that apply to each picture.

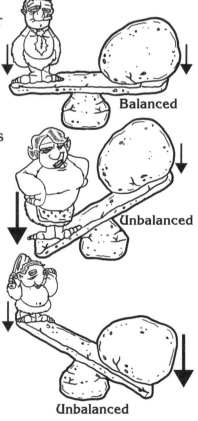

Balanced

Unbalanced

Unbalanced

BALANCED AND UNBALANCED FORCES

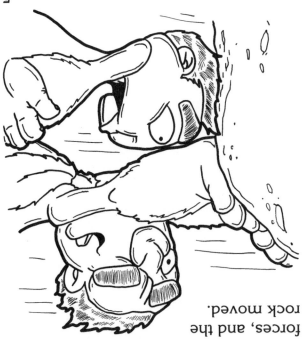

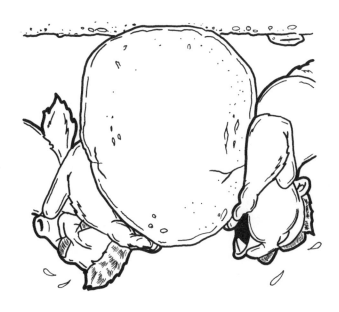

When the two pushed together from the same side, the force to move the rock was greater than the force of gravity that was holding it in place. There were unbalanced forces, and the rock moved.

When Ug and Squirl were pushing on the opposite sides of the rock, they had a balanced force. The force from each side was equal so they cancelled each other out.

Later that day Ug challenged Squirl to an arm-wrestling contest. With some effort, Ug was able to beat Squirl. Feeling quite confident, he challenged Hoam. Hoam soundly beat Ug.

Hoam showed Ug and Squirl a large rock she wanted moved out of their cave. Ug pushed from one side and Squirl pushed from the other side. They could not move it at all. Hoam persuaded Ug to move to the same side of the rock as Squirl. They pushed together and were able to move the rock with ease.

Newton's Third Law says:

> "Every action has an equal and opposite reaction."

Let's say you are standing on your skateboard. If you jump off the front of it (action), the skateboard moves backward (reaction).

You jump one way, the skateboard moves the opposite way. This demonstrates Newton's Third Law.

Now do the investigation. When you are finished, answer this question.

Would you agree or disagree that your Hero engine was an example of Newton's Third Law? Explain.

Part One

Make a Hero engine.

- Punch four holes.
- Slant holes same direction.
- Hook line on pop top lever.
- Fill can with water.
- Hold can up with string.

Fill in the data table.

Trial	Number of Spins
1	
2	
3	

Average: _____

Imagine this is the top-down view of your Hero engine. Use lines to represent the direction of the water and an arrow to show the direction the can turns.

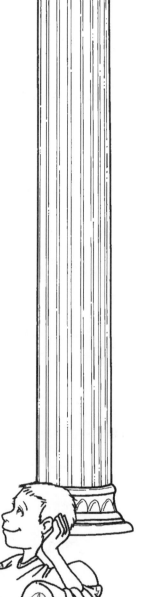

Use your Science Journal to explain in your own words why the can spins.

Part Two

Collect and record your data.

Can 1—Hole Diameters

_____ mm

_____ mm

_____ mm

_____ mm

Average Diameter

_____ mm

Trial	# of Spins
1	
2	
3	

Average: _____

Can 2—Hole Diameters

_____ mm

_____ mm

_____ mm

_____ mm

Average Diameter

_____ mm

Trial	# of Spins
1	
2	
3	

Average: _____

Can 3—Hole Diameters

_____ mm

_____ mm

_____ mm

_____ mm

Average Diameter

_____ mm

Trial	# of Spins
1	
2	
3	

Average: _____

Graph the data.

Number of Spins

Average diameter
of hole (in mm)

Use your Science Journal to write your conclusions about the relationship of the size of the holes and the number of spins. Write a hypothesis using these variables and test it.

The Great Balloon Race

1. Draw a diagram of the race course.

2. Record the time it took your group to complete the course.

3. What two quantities affected the movement of your balloon?

4. Make a table that shows the time it took for each group in the class to complete the course. Include a title and labels for the columns. Put a star next to the group with the fastest time.

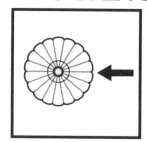

TUG TEAMS

Tug Team Rules

How *do* balanced and unbalanced forces affect the motion of an object?

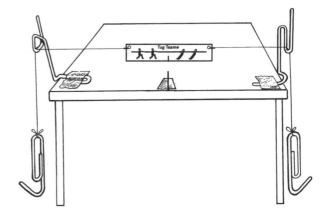

- Set up apparatus as shown.
- Use the weight of a paper clip to represent one unit of force called a **Tugger.** (Weight is a force!)

 = Tugger

- Starter: Center the *Tug Teams* strip over the mark on the masking tape.

First Observation

Put 2 Tuggers on the left hook and 2 Tuggers on the right hook.

On the basis of your observation, answer these questions.

_____ = Number of Tuggers pulling on left side

_____ = Number of Tuggers pulling on right side

Are the Tuggers balanced or unbalanced? _____

Why (<, =, >)? _____

TUG TEAMS
Second Observation

- Starter: Tightly hold the *Tug Teams* strip until directed to let go.
- Left Team Captain: Hang three Tuggers on the left-side hook.

_____ = Number of Tuggers pulling on left side

_____ = Number of Tuggers pulling on right side

Are the Tuggers balanced or unbalanced? _____ Why (<, =, >)? _____

- Predict: The *Tug Teams* strip will: (circle your prediction)

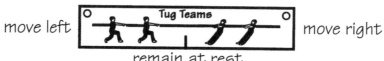

move left   move right

remain at rest

- Starter: Release the *Tug Teams* strip.

What happened? _____ Why? _____

TUG TEAMS
Third Observation

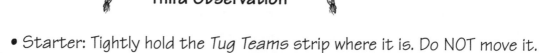

- Starter: Tightly hold the *Tug Teams* strip where it is. Do NOT move it.
- Right Team Captain: Hang three Tuggers on the right-side hook.

_____ = Number of Tuggers pulling on left side

_____ = Number of Tuggers pulling on right side

- Predict: The *Tug Teams* strip will: (circle your prediction)

move left   move right

remain at rest

- Starter: Release the *Tug Teams* strip.

What happened? _____ Why? _____

◀ Paper Airplane Pattern ▶

Folding Instructions:

1. Fold the paper in half along the dashed center line so that the printed side is facing out.

2. Cut along the solid lines.

3. Unfold the paper and fold the left edge over so that it touches the first line. Fold that edge over to meet the next line and so on until you reach the last line.

Celebrating A Century of Flight

4. Fold in half again along the dashed line so that the folded front edge of the wings is on the inside.

5. Fold one wing down along the line that runs parallel to the center.

6. Repeat with the other wing.

7. Open up the airplane. Hold the nose of the airplane level and gently throw. Cut along the dashed lines to make ailerons and elevators to gain more control.

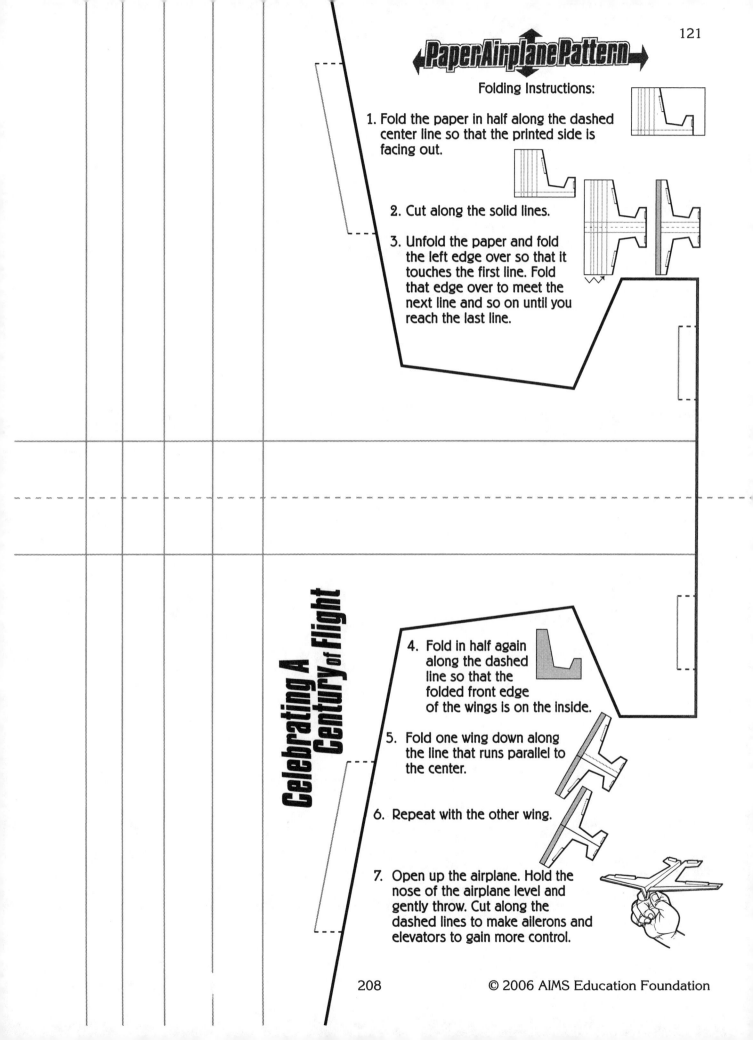

123

Label the four forces acting on your paper airplane in flight.

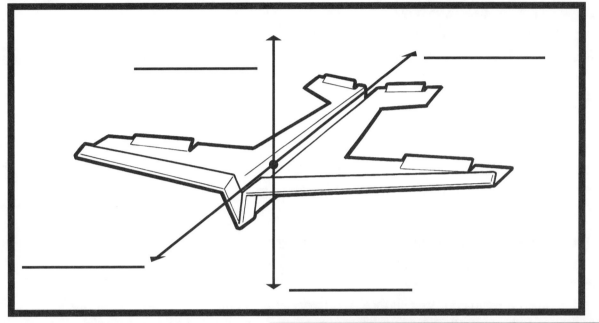

Describe the best flight your airplane made.

A Wing On A String

This simple airfoil can be made with a piece of paper, some string, a quarter-inch hole punch, and a quarter-inch plastic drinking straw. Fold the paper lengthwise so that one edge overlaps the other by about half a centimeter and crease.

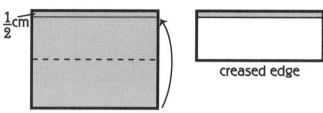

$\frac{1}{2}$ cm

creased edge

Find a horizontal center of the paper (the fore-aft centerline) and mark a point on it a few centimeters from the creased edge. Use a quarter-inch hole punch or sharp pencil to make a hole at the point.

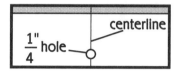

centerline

$\frac{1}{4}$" hole

Bring the two open edges together and tape them. This will cause the paper to bulge a bit in the middle and take the shape of a wing. The shorter side of the paper becomes the flat bottom of the wing and longer side becomes the curved upper surface. The folded edge is the front of the wing and is called the leading edge. The taped edge is the back, or trailing edge, of the wing.

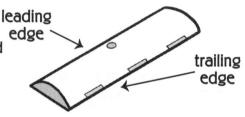

leading edge

trailing edge

Cut a five to six centimeter piece of straw and carefully poke it through the hole in the wing. Center the straw in the wing and secure it with a piece of transparent tape. To prevent the tape from changing the shape of the airfoil, cut it so that it wraps snugly around the straw.

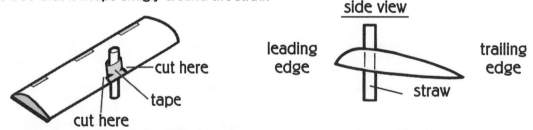

cut here

tape

cut here

side view

leading edge

trailing edge

straw

Cut a piece of string about 50 cm long and thread it through the straw. Cut the remaining length of straw in half and tie the pieces to the string as handles. Secure the string to the handles with tape. The wing is now ready to be tested! Go outside with the wing on a windy day and hold the string taut by the handles with the leading edge facing into the wind. It may be necessary to hold the wing with the leading edge angled up slightly. If it isn't windy enough outside, walk briskly in a straight line or spin around with it. As air goes around the wing, it should rise up on the string demonstrating lift, the same force that allows planes to fly.

lift

airflow

When the Leas could not move the animals, the forces of gravity and friction were greater than the force pushing them. When Ug and Squirl pushed just the saber-toothed tiger instead of both pets, the mass they were trying to push was less. Hoam joined in with Wooly, so that they increased their pushing force.

Ug tried to push both of the family pets out of the cave at the same time. He pushed and pushed and pushed. They did not move at all.

Newton, a 17th century English scientist/mathematician, said that the movement of an object depends on the object's mass and how much force is applied to it. He would be proud that the Leas learned that a change of force or a change in mass affects the motion of an object.

NEWTON'S 2ND LAW According to the Lea Family

Hoam wanted to clean the cave. This meant that a reluctant pet saber-toothed tiger and wooly mammoth needed to be moved.

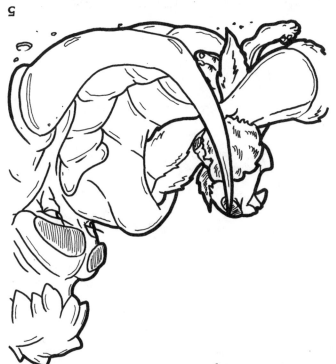

Pleased with their success they began pushing on Wooly. They pushed and pushed and pushed. They could not move Wooly at all.

Hoam motioned for them to try pushing just the saber-toothed tiger. They pushed, and the cat was soon out of the cave.

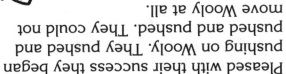

Hoam joined her family. They all pushed. With their combined effort, they were able to push Wooly out of the cave.

He grunted for Squirl to help. They both pushed and pushed and pushed. The animals did not move at all.

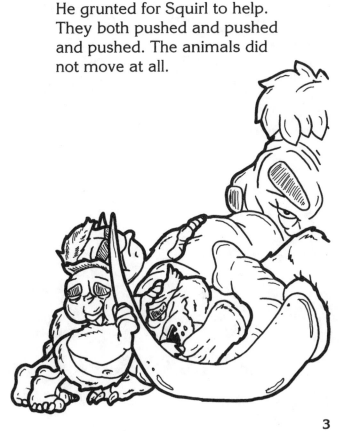

Balancing Your Clustered Balloons

1. Describe the process you used to balance your clustered balloons.

2. Identify and describe the "up" and "down" forces acting on the cluster balloons.

   The "up" force:

   The "down" force:

3. Draw a free-body diagram of cluster balloons at the time that you balanced the forces

Cluster Balloon Flight

Free-body Diagram

Balancing Your Clustered Balloons

CLUSTER BALLOONING

Complete the free-body diagram and record whether the cluster balloon is rising, decending, or balanced.

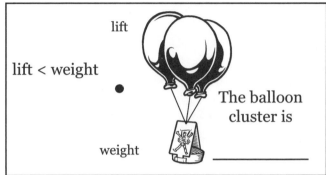

lift < weight

The balloon cluster is

_____

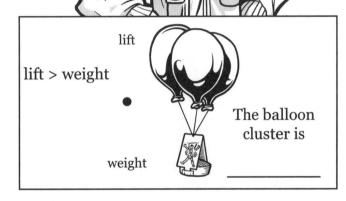

lift > weight

The balloon cluster is

_____

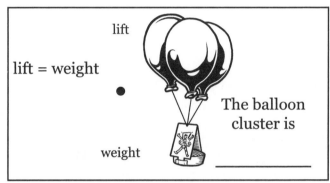

lift = weight

The balloon cluster is

_____

Complete the free-body diagram and use the correct relation symbol (=, >, or <) that describes each cluster balloon flight.

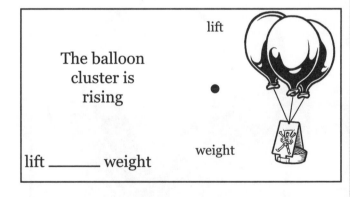

The balloon cluster is rising

lift _____ weight

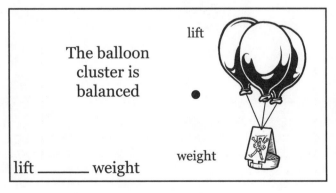

The balloon cluster is balanced

lift _____ weight

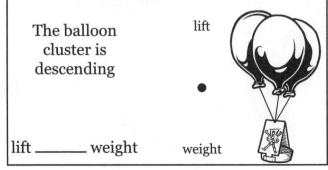

The balloon cluster is descending

lift _____ weight

Memo On Motion

(Position, Direction, and Speed)

The motion of an object can be described by its position, the direction it is moving, as well as its speed. When you see an object that appears to be moving, you know that it is changing its position relative to where you are.

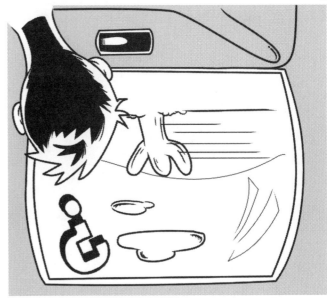

Think about riding in a car. Let's say you are traveling north at 60 miles an hour. If you look out the passenger window, objects appear to be moving by quickly. They appear to move relative to your position in the car. The car is moving, not the objects.

You notice other cars on the road. Some are traveling north, some are traveling south. The cars traveling north are going in the same direction as you are. Cars that are traveling south appear to move faster. Cars that are traveling north appear to be moving slower.

Motion is a change in position. Direction is relative to some fixed place or object. Speed is a measurement of that change in position over time.

MOTION:
CHANGE IN POSITION.

DIRECTION:
RELATIVE TO SOME
FIXED PLACE.

SPEED:
MEASUREMENT OF TH
CHANGE IN P
OVER TIME.

Name_____

1. Record the position of the car at each time interval. If you land on a position that causes you to lose time, record a zero in the Roll column.

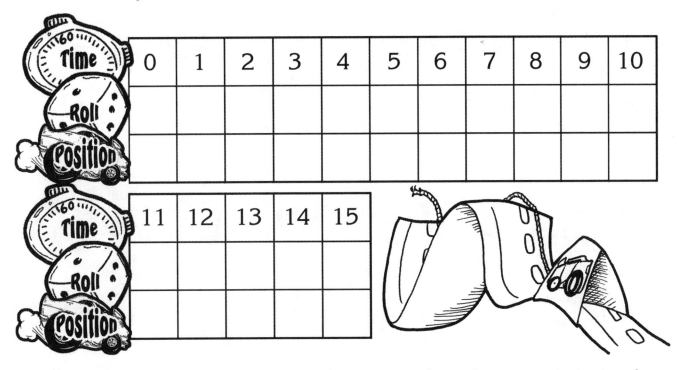

Time	0	1	2	3	4	5	6	7	8	9	10
Roll											
Position											

Time	11	12	13	14	15
Roll					
Position					

2. Using the data table as a record of your trip, describe your trip in words.

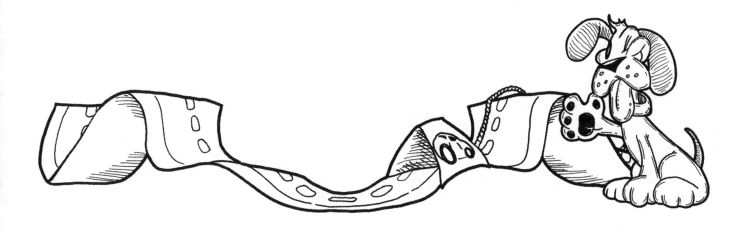

Name_____

Time to Move It!

3. Graph the data.

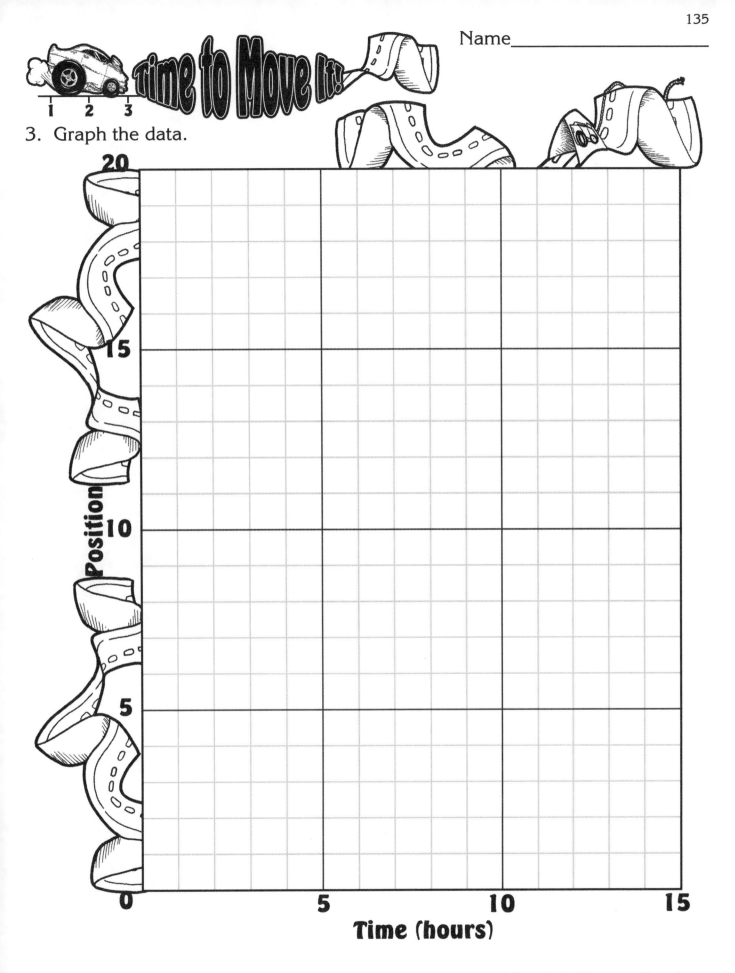

Position

20

15

10

5

0   5   10   15

Time (hours)

4. The graph shows the data for a friend's trip. From the graph, describe in detail the events of your friend's trip.

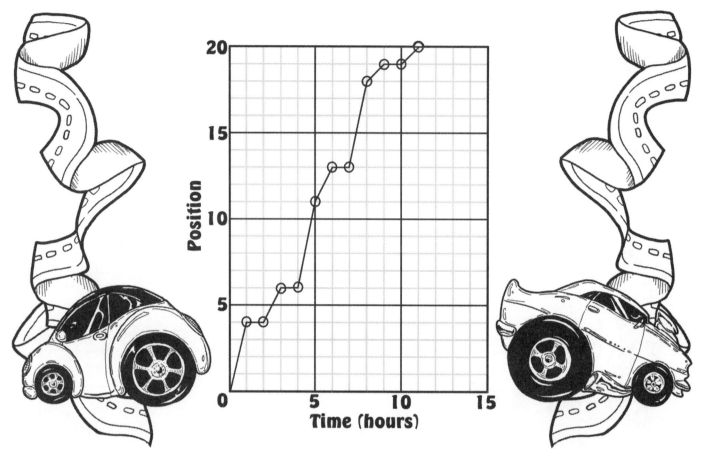

Name_____

1. Record the position of the car at each time interval. If you land on a position that causes you to lose time, record a zero in the Roll column.

Time	0	1	2	3	4	5	6	7	8	9	10
Roll											
Position											

Time	11	12	13	14	15	16	17	18	19	20	21
Roll											
Position											

2. Using the data table as a record of your trip, describe your trip in words.

Name_____

Time to Move It More!

3. Graph the data.

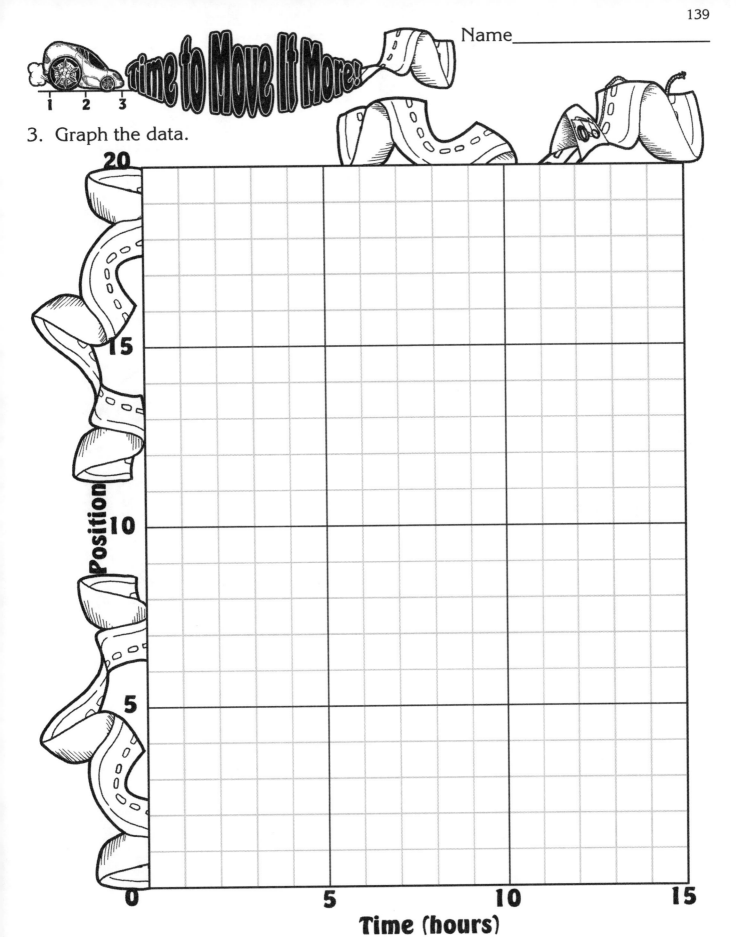

Position

Time (hours)

Name_____

4. The graph shows the data for a friend's trip. From the graph, describe in detail the events of your friend's trip.

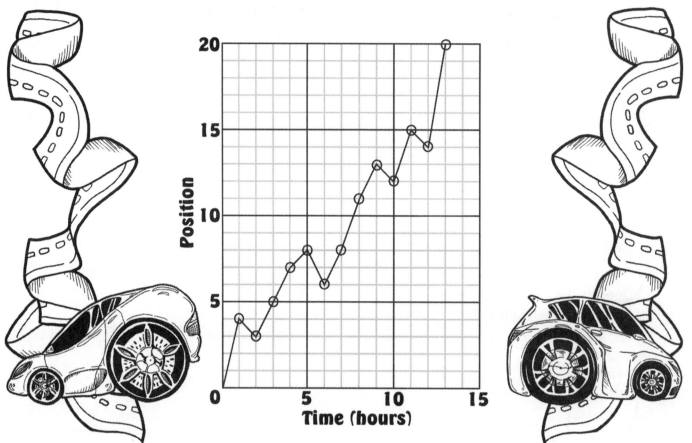

Bouncing Around

Select a ball and surface to which it will be dropped. Let it fall the distances shown 3 times from each height. Measure the highest point of each bounce and find the average. Before making the first drop, predict how high the ball will bounce if dropped 100 centimeters.

#1

Prediction:	Type of ball:	Type of Surface:

Falling distance in centimeters		100	80	60	40	20
Height of bounce in centimeters	Trial #1					
	Trial #2					
	Trial #3					
	Sum					
	Average					

Write a formula relating B to h.
B = height of bounce
h = height of drop

B =   h

#2

Prediction:	Type of ball:	Type of Surface:

Falling distance in centimeters		100	80	60	40	20
Height of bounce in centimeters	Trial #1					
	Trial #2					
	Trial #3					
	Sum					
	Average					

Write a formula relating B to h.
B = height of bounce
h = height of drop

B =   h

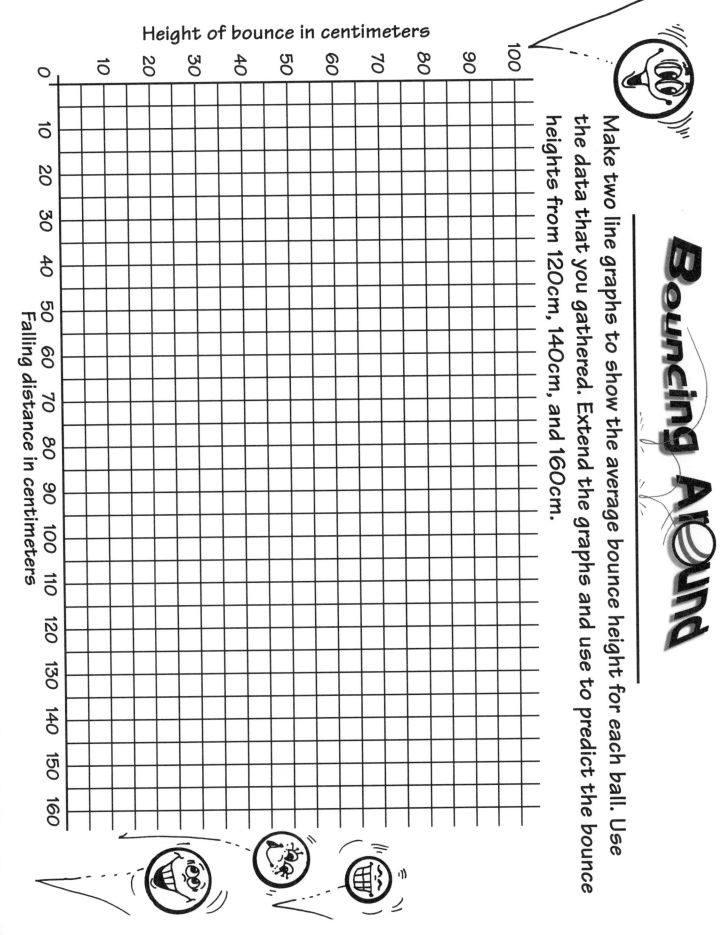

Bouncing Around

Make two line graphs to show the average bounce height for each ball. Use the data that you gathered. Extend the graphs and use to predict the bounce heights from 120cm, 140cm, and 160cm.

Height of bounce in centimeters

Falling distance in centimeters

Clock Your Walk

1. Record the distance in meters between the *Start* line and the *Finish* line.
2. For each of three trials, record the time it took you to walk the measured distance.
3. For each of your three trials, compute your velocity in feet per second. Use the relationship, *average velocity equals distance divided by time.*

Data	Time (seconds)	Distance (meters)
Trial One		
Trial Two		
Trial Three		

$$\text{average velocity} = \frac{\text{distance}}{\text{time}}$$

TICK! TICK!

Trial 1	average velocity = _____	$\dfrac{\text{meters}}{\text{seconds}}$ =	_____	meters per second
Trial 2	average velocity = _____	$\dfrac{\text{meters}}{\text{seconds}}$ =	_____	meters per second
Trial 3	average velocity = _____	$\dfrac{\text{meters}}{\text{seconds}}$ =	_____	meters per second

4. What's your fastest walking velocity in meters per second?

PULL OVER! YOU'RE WALKING TOO FAST, SON!

5. Put a star beside your fastest average walking velocity.

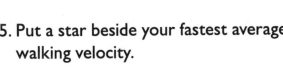

Clock Your Walk

6. Record your fastest average walking velocity here. walking average velocity = $\dfrac{\text{meters}}{\text{seconds}}$

Time (seconds)	0	1	2	3	4	5	6	7	8	9	10
Distance (meters)											

7. Use your best walking average velocity (the distance you can walk in one second) to complete the table.

8. Graph the data in the table.

9. Project your graph to the edge of the grid.

10. At your walking average velocity, how far could you walk in 15 seconds?

...in 1 minute?

...in 10 minutes?

...in one hour?

...in one day?

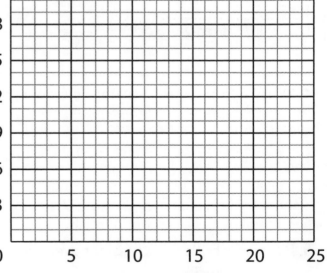

HOLD'ER STEADY, BOY!

CLEAN ALL

Distance (meters) — 3, 6, 9, 12, 15, 18, 21, 24, 27, 30, 33, 36, 39, 42, 45, 48, 51

Time (seconds) — 5, 10, 15, 20, 25

A variable is something you can change. There are three basic types of variables.
- variables that you change,
- variables that you keep the same, and
- variables that are a result of what happens in the investigation.

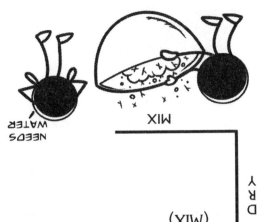

NEEDS WATER   MIX   DRY

- Manipulated Independent X-axis (MIX)
- Dependent, Responding, Y-axis (DRY)

of the variables is: DRY MIX. (DRY) good way to remember the placement Height is the responding variable. A along the vertical axis. The Bounce variable. The Bounce Height is plotted Height is the manipulated (independent) along the horizontal axis. The Drop The data for the Drop Height is plotted

I AM THE GREAT AND MYSTERIOUS VARIABLE! I COME IN VARIOUS FORMS AND WILL AMAZE YOU AND FRUSTRATE YOU, ALL AT THE SAME TIME!!

OOOHH   AAAHHH

Graphically Speaking

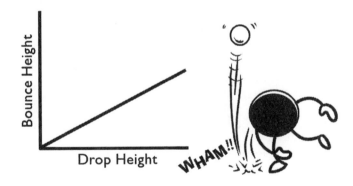

Bounce Height

Drop Height

WHAM!!

The graph shows a relationship. The higher you dropped the ball, the higher it bounced. You can tell this just by looking at the graph. A straight slope on a graph shows a consistent relationship. A curved slope or a broken line on a graph does not show that consistency. Read each of the following graphs and describe the motion the graph is showing.

Variables that you change are called *manipulated* variables. They are also called independent variables. Let's say you wanted to find out how drop height affects the bounce height of a super ball. You would try dropping the ball from different heights. The different heights you test are what you changed. The manipulated variable is the X value on a graph. It is placed on the horizontal axis.

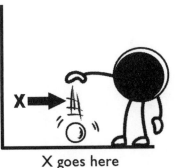

X goes here

© 2006 AIMS Education Foundation

Responding variables are what happens when something is changed. The super balls bounce when they are dropped. The different bounce heights are the responding variable. Responding variables are also called dependent variables. The responding variable is the Y value on a graph. It is placed on the vertical axis.

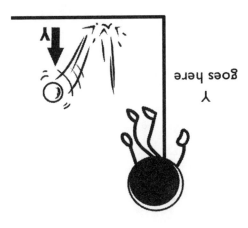

Y goes here

4

The other variables are called *controlled* variables. These are all the conditions that you try to keep the same so that it is a fair test. In an investigation on super balls, you would need to use the same type of super ball on the same surface. These would be controlled variables.

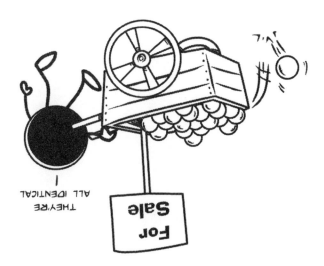

For Sale

THEY'RE ALL IDENTICAL

5

One purpose of a graph is to show relationships between data. A graph shows trends and patterns better than a data table alone. Each point on a graph represents a pair of data. The value for the X-axis is listed first. It uses the horizontal axis. The y-value is second. It uses the Y-axis.

(100, 72)

Graphically Speaking

I PREDICT THE VARIABLE WILL BE YOUR HORRIBLE AIM.

SMACK

OOPS!

Tell the stories of the graphs.

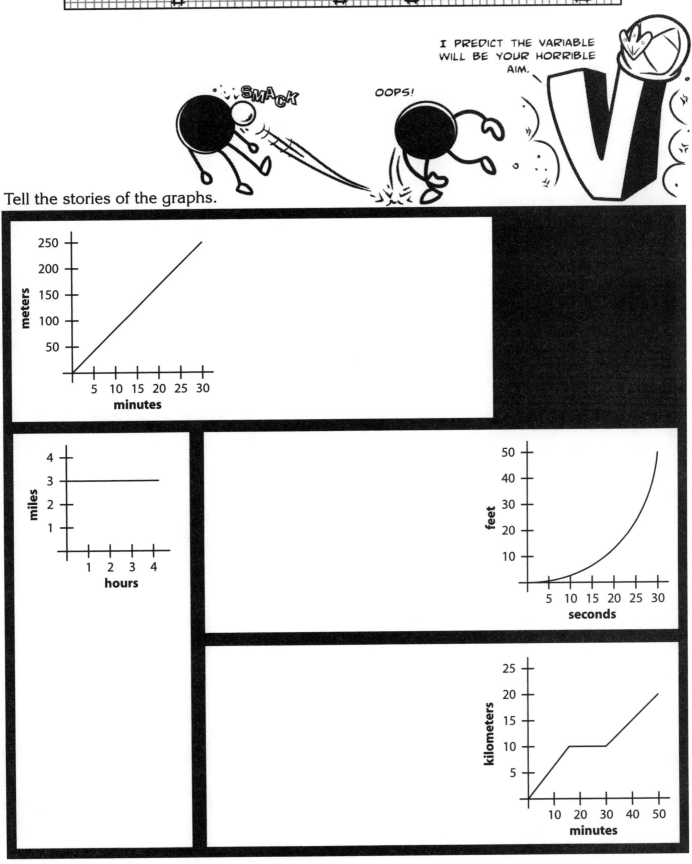

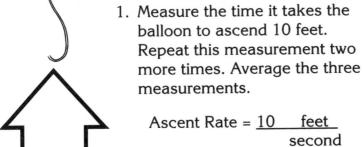

1. Measure the time it takes the balloon to ascend 10 feet. Repeat this measurement two more times. Average the three measurements.

Ascent Rate = $\dfrac{10 \quad \text{feet}}{\text{second}}$

Ascent Rate = $\dfrac{\text{feet}}{1 \quad \text{second}}$

Distance (feet)		10
Time (seconds)	1	
	2	
	3	
Average		

2. Use the average ascent rate to complete the table.

Time	0	1	2	3	4	5	6
Distance							

3. Graph the data in the table.

4. Add a title to your graph.

Distance (feet)

Time (seconds)

0 1 2 3 4 5 6 7 8 9 10

How Heavy? GO! How Far?

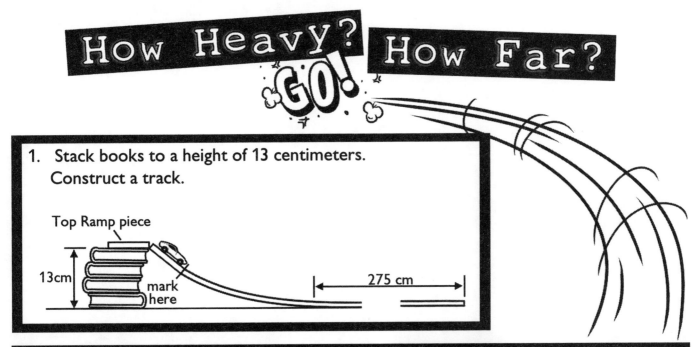

1. Stack books to a height of 13 centimeters. Construct a track.

Top Ramp piece

13cm

mark here

275 cm

2. For each of three trials, measure and record the distance in centimeters your car travels along the straight track. Measure from the bottom of the track to the front of the car. If your car runs off the track, measure along a straight line from the track to the front of your car.

	Distance Traveled
Trial 1	
Trial 2	
Trial 3	
Average	

VVVROOOM...

3. Talk to your classmates and find a car that has less mass than your car and record its *Average Distance*. Find a car that has more mass than your car and record its *Average Distance*.

	Your Car	Lighter Car	Heavier Car
Mass:			
	Mass:	Mass:	Mass:
	Average Distance:	Average Distance:	Average Distance:

4. Explain what effect you think the variable *mass* has on the distance the toy car travels down the track.

Push to
START

track   launcher   toy car   distance traveled

1. Predict the relationship between the *Force Level* at which a car is pushed and the distance the car travels down the track.

2. For each of the *Force Levels*, measure the distance your car travels down the track. Complete three trials at each *Force Level* and average the results. Record the measurement data and computed averages in the table.

Mass of car = _____ grams

Data	Trial One	Trial Two	Trial Three	
	Distance (cm)	Distance (cm)	Distance (cm)	Average (cm)
Force level 0				
Force level 1				
Force level 2				
Force level 3				
Force level 4				
Force level 5				
Force level 6				

3. Graph the *Force Level—Average Distance* data.

YEEHAW!

4. Describe the general relationship between the *Force Level* and the distance the car traveled as shown by your graph.

5. Compare your prediction to what is shown in your graph.

6. Find a car with a mass at least 10 grams more than your car. Record and graph its *Average Distance* data.

mass of car = _____ grams

Data	Average Distance (cm)
Force level 0	
Force level 1	
Force level 2	
Force level 3	
Force level 4	
Force level 5	
Force level 6	

Average Distance (cm)

Force level

0 1 2 3 4 5 6

Key
☐ My car
☐ Greater mass
☐ Less mass

7. Find a car with a mass at least 10 grams less than your car. Record and graph its *Average Distance* data.

mass of car = _____ grams

Data	Average Distance (cm)
Force level 0	
Force level 1	
Force level 2	
Force level 3	
Force level 4	
Force level 5	
Force level 6	

8. Does your graph show any relationship between the masses of the cars and the *Average Distances* traveled? If so, describe the relationship.

THE BIG BOPPER

Safety Requirement:
Every student must
wear safety goggles.

Force – Distance Data

Force 1	_____	centimeters
Force 1	_____	centimeters
Average	_____	centimeters
Force 2	_____	centimeters
Force 2	_____	centimeters
Average	_____	centimeters
Force 3	_____	centimeters
Force 3	_____	centimeters
Average	_____	centimeters
Force 4	_____	centimeters
Force 4	_____	centimeters
Average	_____	centimeters

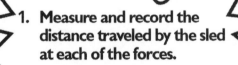

1. **Measure and record the distance traveled by the sled at each of the forces.**

2. **Graph the average distance of each of the forces.**

3. **Describe the relationship between the Force applied to the sled and the distance traveled by the sled.**

4. **Put a title on your graph.**

OUCH.

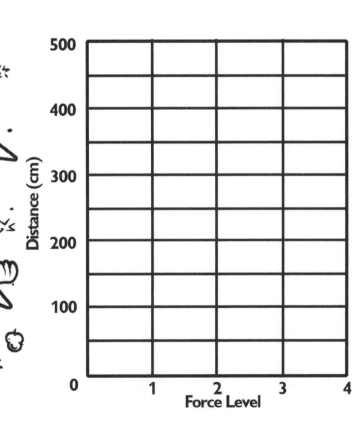

Dr. John Paul Stapp

Colonel,
United States Air Force
1910 - 1999

You know that the first thing to do when you get into a car is to buckle your seat belt and shoulder harness.

You also know from TV commercials that Vince and Larry are two crash test dummies. Their funny antics remind you to always "buckle up."

Both the seat belt and crash dummy were pioneered by a United States Air Force doctor. His name is Dr. John Stapp and he is known as the Rocket Doctor.

Dr. Stapp wanted to find out why some Air Force pilots lived and others died as a result of similar crashes. Was it the forces from the crash itself or was there another explanation?

To answer this question, he built a rocket-powered sled called Gee Whiz. Gee Whiz rode on tracks like a train. Speeding up and slowing down, the sled created forces like those in an airplane crash.

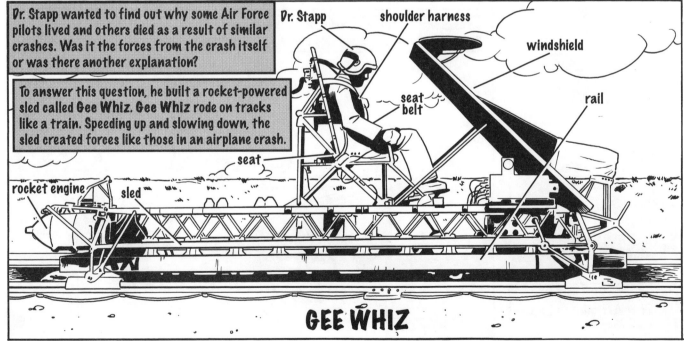

GEE WHIZ

Dr. Stapp and his team built a crash dummy they named Oscar. Oscar's job was to test pilot seats, seat belts, and shoulder harnesses. Oscar rode the rocket sled 32 times before Dr. Stapp decided the seat and safety harness was ready for a human to test.

In 1947, Dr. Stapp was the first human to ride the rocket sled. He rode the sled for almost two miles at speeds up to 200 miles per hour.

The brakes on the sled stopped the sled in 19 feet!

THAT'S FAST.

His tests showed that the human body could survive most airplane crashes. But the pilot's seat had to be strong enough not to break loose and the pilot's body had to be strapped down.

When airplanes started flying faster than the speed of sound (above 700 miles per hour), new safety problems arose.

If some part of the airplane failed, could a pilot bail out at such a speed?

Dr. Stapp built a second rocket sled, the **Sonic Wind No.1**, to study this problem.

Oscar, the crash dummy, was once again the first to ride the **Sonic Wind.**

Once tests were completed, Dr. Stapp made his first ride on the sled. He set a new land speed record of 421 miles per hour.

A year later, Dr. Stapp was rocketed to a speed of 623 miles per hour in 5 seconds. The sled was stopped in one and one-quarter second.

For a short time, his body weight became 6800 pounds.

The work of Dr. Stapp and his team led to the systems pilots now use if they have to crash or leave the airplane at high speed.

In 1967, he began to study car accidents. He made the first automobile crash tests that used crash dummies. Out of these tests came the seat belts, padded dashboards, and air bags found in every new car.

"A lot of people from around the world—both pilots and car drivers—owe their lives to the pioneering work of Dr. Stapp."

-Dr. James Young
Chief Historian
Air Force Flight
Test Center

Edwards Air
Force Base,
California

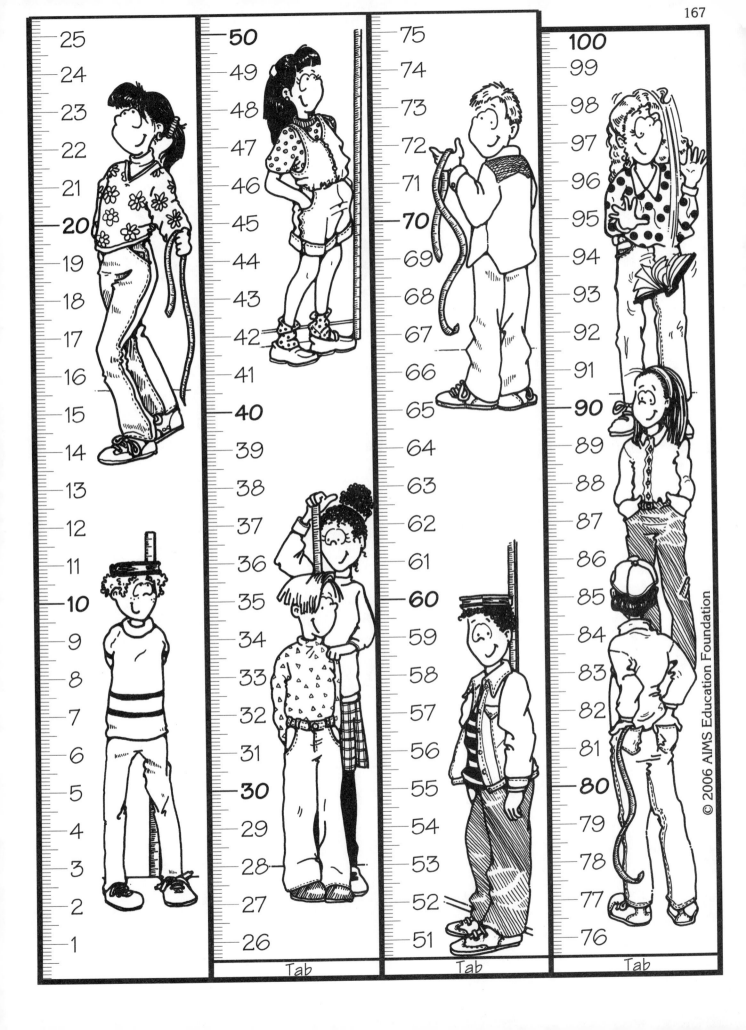

167

© 2006 AIMS Education Foundation

Tab   Tab   Tab